IS THERE NOT A CAUSE?

Is There Not A Cause?
Beyond the Disappointment
of Aimless Christianity

Joseph Tosini

CITYHILL PUBLISHING
Columbia, Missouri

Is There Not A Cause?
Beyond the Disappointment
of Aimless Christianity

Joseph Tosini

ISBN 0-939159-17-1

Printed in the U.S.A.
Cityhill Publishing
4600 Christian Fellowship Road
Columbia, Missouri U.S.A. 65203

DEDICATION

The cover of this book bears my name; the contents bear the hearts of the precious men, women, and children who are joined together in a local church called Christian Fellowship of Columbia. To each of them, especially the children, who will one day take our place, this book is affectionately dedicated.

CONTENTS

SECTION THREE: THE BARRIERS

THANKS

It is 7:08 a.m. In one hour, the completed manuscript will be on its way to the typesetter. All that is needed are the acknowledgements.

This morning marks the end of a fifteen-day marathon to complete this manuscript. Each of the last five days we have had the privilege of seeing the sun rise before going to sleep for a few hours. This ordeal might help clarify what we mean by "team effort."

This project was spearheaded by Bob Briggs, who oversees Cityhill Publishing, the publications ministry of our church, and assisted by editor Dick Myhre and production coordinator Frank Pierce. As the deadline for this book drew near, Bob and Dick found a hideaway and had me join them later to make sure we would complete our task. Three days is what they said we would need.

A couple in our church, Gary and Laurel McLagan, who are expecting a child at any moment, just moved into their new house two days before Bob and Dick took over their lower level. As the work intensified, we began staying into the night, and the team increased. An expanding Cityhill crew—Jan, Betty, Ann, and Pam—began working around the clock in the McLagan's basement. Every day for the past week, Bob and I have told our wives the work would be finished "today."

Word spread throughout the church: "The book is almost done. Send food." People began the food runs, and platters of cold cuts, trays of fruit, and full-course meals began appearing. The church's leadership team and others began proofing the manuscript. Twenty people in all—all had suggestions, and all were taken into account. The copyediting team were tested to the limit in their appreciation of their brethren's suggestions. So was Jan Petersen, who designed the cover of this book twice— once just before giving birth to a little boy, then after the birth when the original design looked different to her. Ann Weaver kept everyone calm with her organizational skills and constant words of encouragement: "Don't panic."

I remember Dick telling Frank, "I'm on the edge. Don't push me over." It was 3:30 a.m. This morning, it was reversed. As Dick handed Frank another chapter covered with red ink, Frank said, "That's enough. I've had it. No more changes." Dick believed him. All the while, behind the scenes, our valiant spouses carried on a lonely vigil on the homefront.

The unsung hero, though, is Betty Rodgers, the strongest woman in the world. Her stamina at age 62 outshines us all. I begged her, "*Please* go to bed," right before several of us passed out. When we awoke, Betty had been up for hours, working.

Many times, whether from fatigue or emotional strain, laughter took us to our knees. Even in this hectic wrapup, with pauses for prayer, pretzels, and phone calls home, in the midst of a makeshift editorial office strewn with papers and picnic coolers, we realized that we were living out the message of this book.

INTRODUCTION

The champion fighter of the Philistines strode boldly out of his camp and stood before thousands of Israelites assembled for battle. "I defy the ranks of Israel," Goliath shouted.

The fighting men of Israel were paralyzed with fear, but one voice penetrated their malaise. Facing Goliath's taunts and the armies of the Philistines, a young man with a courageous heart stepped forward. Mocked for his confident zeal, he challenged the warriors of Israel with a stirring question: "Is there not a cause?"[1]

That question, posed by David centuries ago, is still relevant today. It asks of Christians, "Isn't there a purpose worthy of our whole lives? Isn't there a reason for giving everything?"

The odds stacked against the people of God seem as overwhelming as ever. The church seems weak and without vitality. Many believers, especially those who have grown up in a generation hungry for a cause, just don't see the point of it all. The world stands by watching and listening as an aimless people make claims they can't back up. The credibility gap widens. Like in David's day, it is time for the people of God to be reminded that they represent the only hope for a failing world.

I would not have written this book if I did not think that millions of believers have been disappointed, whether by the highly visible failures of contemporary Christianity or by their own personal experiences. I have known my share of that kind of frustration, and my heart goes out to those who have yet to find the clarity of direction they yearn for. But nearly fifteen years ago my frustration began to diminish. I stopped drifting and committed myself to a way of life that, despite its difficulties, has not left me disappointed.

This book does not lay out an easy, several-step formula for spiritual success. It's simply a story about the cause I have found—its biblical foundations, its requirements, and the evidence that it works. I invite you to follow along as this book examines the major themes of the Bible—topics such as loving God, loving people, the church, the cross, the nation of Israel, and the prophetic promises—and see how all the various truths of the Bible fit together perfectly and point to a single, unified goal. By stepping back and looking at the big picture of what God wants to accomplish rather than focusing on isolated pieces of truth, we can identify the central cause of Christianity, which is the purpose for human life.

I'll be straightforward about where this book is heading. First, it conveys my conviction that the message of the Bible can be summarized in a single word: relationship. Those who adopt God's relational way of life—loving Him and one another—will be His family. That family has a name, church, and it is the focus of God's passion and zeal. It should be ours as well. You will also find in this book a strong appeal for commitment to the local church. My view is that it is only within the context of the local church that we can fully live out the content of the kingdom, expressing the heart of God to a watching world.

If by the time you finish reading this book you are not challenged, then I have not succeeded. And if you read this and say, "I know all this; I'm looking for a 'meatier' message," you will have missed the point. If you take offense at some of what I am saying, keep in mind that I am not challenging my brothers and sisters in the Lord, but only the principles by which we operate. I speak frankly about my frustrations over fruitless teaching because I am determined to see a Christianity that lives up to what it proclaims.

This book has sprung not only from my own life, but also from the lives of many other people with whom the Lord has joined me. We have lived out the message you are about to read, and it has changed our lives. By including stories about this church and the people here, it may sound to some like I'm saying, "We've arrived." We have not. But we have stepped beyond the realm of ideas and have tested this message in the laboratory of daily living. That is the evidence I offer, along with a simple picture explaining the Bible. I offer this message and our story in order to stir up hope that the church can work, and that you can invest your best years in a most worthy cause.

IS THERE NOT A CAUSE?

SECTION ONE:

JOURNEY THROUGH THE MAZE

CHAPTER 1

THEOLOGICAL PINBALL

Baseball was my boyhood dream. I lived less than a half-hour's bus ride from Ebbets Field in Brooklyn, N.Y. I remember my father taking me to a Dodger game when I was about eight years old. We arrived early to watch the teams warm up. I stood behind the fence, just a few feet away from the Dodger's catcher, Roy Campanella, who was handling the blazing fastballs of a new eighteen-year-old pitching sensation, Sandy Koufax.

I loved it, and I imagined that I could be out there someday. Starting out as a little leaguer, I climbed on the pitcher's mound and pitched for a team every year until I was eighteen. I had a single goal: to play professional baseball. That was my cause. I was devoted to it. I thought about it, talked about it, dreamed about it.

My prospects were promising; professional scouts who periodically dropped by were optimistic about my chances, and I had enough success to boost my confidence that my dream would come to pass. But the summer after I graduated from high school, the unexpected happened. As I whipped my arm around to deliver my hardest fastball, the tendons ripped in my shoulder. With one pitch, in one brief moment, my dream was over. I would never throw a good fastball again. For so many years my heart had been set on the major leagues; but my vision vanished, and in its place was the ache of disappointment.

Search through the '60s

Wandering through the next few years, I searched for something
of significance. Making money, climbing the ladder of success,
and striving for status seemed like such empty goals. Around me
I saw a world in violent confusion. It was the late 1960s, a
tumultuous time when the undercurrents of rebellion seemed to
be shaking the foundational values of our culture. Bold challenges
to basic values and institutions served as a catalyst for an entire
generation of young people to begin asking a lot of questions.
This questioning left us open for some new answers, at least
different answers from what our parents' generation was offering
us. As a result new causes emerged, enlisting the devotion of
many disillusioned young people.

Songwriters were giving directions back then, posing questions
and stirring emotions. Bob Dylan, described by many as the
major prophet of the day, promoted a breaking away from the
values and institutions that molded our lives. "The times they are
a-changin'," he announced:

> *Come mothers and fathers throughout the land.*
> *Don't criticize what you can't understand.*
> *Your sons and your daughters are beyond your command.*
> *Your old world is rapidly fading.*
> *Please get out of the new one if you can't lend a hand,*
> *For the times they are a-changin'.*[1]

The battle outside was raging, Dylan warned government
leaders, and "he who gets hurt will be he who stalls—for the
times they are a-changin'." His lyrics spurred many into action,
and like-minded radicals began assembling on the West Coast.
Another song spoke of that emerging movement:

> *If you're going to San Francisco,*
> *You're sure to find some gentle people there . . . .*
> *All across the nation,*

Such a strange vibration, people in motion . . . .
There's a whole generation with a new explanation.²

The lyrics made me start wondering what it would be like on the West Coast, where thousands of these would-be world changers were gathering. Intrigued, I headed across the continent to San Francisco to see this new cause for myself. I arrived in the Haight-Ashbury district, where the buildings were painted in bright colors and young people were dressed in beads and bandanas. As I got out of my car I saw a startling-looking girl, about eighteen years old. With long, flowing blond hair and in a paisley dress, she was standing on a corner handing out vanilla wafers to passers-by. I took one.

"Why are you doing this?" I asked her.

She looked in my eyes, and with a big smile, she summed up the theme of a whole movement.

"Love," she said.

Standing there a few minutes munching on my wafer, I took in more of the scene. Something significant, I thought to myself, is happening here.

My new home was an apartment over a Chinese laundry in Berkeley, the hotbed of radicalism. Just two blocks from the University of California campus, my two roommates and I were planted right in the middle of the oddest combination of people you could imagine. We lived just above some people involved with the Students for a Democratic Society, or SDS, and a gang of "Hell's Angels" hung around on the corner.

Enthusiastically I immersed myself in this new cause, a California lifestyle that promoted peace and love. As time went by, though, what had started out so fresh and invigorating began losing its edge. Finally, within the course of a single week, some events took place that shook me badly.

The first blow came when I learned of two drug-related murders near my apartment. Popular songs encouraged people to "turn on" to drugs. Drugs represented freedom and opened the door to this new brand of love and peace. During demonstrations against the war in Vietnam, throngs of young people would link arms, sway together, and sing in unison about a world without war. Well, we were dreaming of peace, but people were still getting gunned down—over drugs. The people who were championing the peace movement were killing each other. I started wondering what was happening.

A few days later, I was walking down the street in the evening to get an ice cream cone when a girl no more than thirteen or fourteen approached me. She had the Janis Joplin look, with long stringy hair and ragged clothes. Desperate for drugs, she asked for money. I looked at her, listened to her pleas, and became deeply distressed. I could see that this girl's life was in ruins. She had run away from home, "escaping" to this mecca of idealism only to get hooked on drugs. I wondered if she had parents who cared about her. I wanted to help her but couldn't. In a wild-eyed panic, she pushed me away and ran down the street, sobbing. For days I couldn't erase from my mind the picture of that girl's anguished face.

I did a lot of thinking about what we were doing. Whatever it was, it wasn't working. I had come with the naive notion that the California dream would take people beyond the violent, perverse, hate-filled society I wanted to leave behind. But two dead bodies in a week and a devastated runaway tore some gaping holes in my outlook. I began to see that the counterculture movement was polluted with the same corruption and greed as the society it was trying to change; that despite all its promises, the vision of a new society was crushed in the vise of selfishness and pride. Yet another cause of mine was collapsing. Again I was left disappointed.

On my knees

In the midst of all this confusion another voice was calling me. Through some student friends of mine, I met someone who talked to me about Jesus. For me, religion had always been boring, lifeless, and irrelevant. But I had never before heard anybody talk like this person did. I ended up going to church and hearing about a born-again salvation experience in which God could actually change your heart.

More than a year had passed after I first heard that message when one evening I found myself sitting in on a revival service. We sang a few songs before the evangelist started preaching. I listened for a while; then my mind started wandering. I was not sure I believed anything I had been told; I was not even sure if God existed, but I wanted to know. After the service, while people were milling around talking to their friends, I had a strong urge to pray.

There was something I did believe: I knew that the whole world was afflicted with a terribly disabling disease that nobody could cure, and I knew I had that disease because it seemed that everything I did and desired was selfish. I sat there thinking about the things I was doing that hurt other people. I was deeply sorry. I knew, though, that I couldn't change myself. I found a place at the front of the church where I could be alone, and I knelt. Even as I did I felt stupid, yet I had to know if Jesus was real. I uttered the most sincere words I'd ever spoken in my life. I apologized to God for my behavior and told him how deeply sorry I was for the kind of person I had been.

As I prayed, I felt a hand on my shoulder. I assumed someone had noticed me and had come to pray with me. I turned to see who it was, but there wasn't a person within twenty feet of me. I began to cry. I knew it had to have been God responding to my prayer by touching me. I'll never forget that moment. The pressure of God's hand on my shoulder was as real as the floor I was kneeling on. Equally real was the knowledge that I had a choice to make: I could say "Leave me alone," or I could allow Jesus to take command of my life. I surrendered.

Then I felt that hand sweep through my whole body. I knew that Jesus had entered my heart and that I would never be the same. I still do not know why God showed such mercy to me, forgiving me and revealing Himself to me in such a dramatic fashion; but I do know that He rescued me from disaster by setting me on a different path—His path.

With the zeal of a new convert, I plunged into my new cause at a breakneck pace. I had found the truth and became determined to share it with everyone who would listen, even with those who would not. I prayed incessantly and talked for hours on end with my new friends about the Bible. I was ready to embrace every exciting message that came through the church. But I was in for a number of disillusioning experiences: many of the Christian causes I adopted left me as disappointed as baseball and Berkeley had.

Rapturemania

Because I had so many questions about the Bible, the leaders of my church encouraged me to go to Bible college. At the time I really had no desire to become a pastor, but I figured it would be good to follow their counsel. So off I went.

When classes began I did not even know where the books of the Bible were, much less what doctrines they supported. When I heard about Saul throwing his spear at David, for all I knew they were both used-car salesmen from Queens. Most of what I knew about Israel came from watching the Cecil B. DeMille version of *The Ten Commandments;* Charlton Heston had been my only Bible teacher. When an instructor would tell us to turn to a certain book in the Bible, the room would suddenly feel terribly warm. While students around me would confidently thumb through their Bibles, I did not even know where to begin looking. Thoroughly embarrassed, I would have to turn to the table of contents.

During the years I was in Bible college, many preachers were emphasizing the imminence of Christ's return to earth, preceded by the "rapture," in which all believers would be suddenly taken up into heaven. There was some disagreement about exactly how this end-times scenario would develop, but all agreed that we would not have a long wait for these events. I absorbed this message and genuinely anticipated being whisked away soon along with the rest of the raptured church.

We eagerly watched current events for indications that end-times prophecy was being fulfilled. Our hopes were stirred by rumors that stones for rebuilding Solomon's Temple in Jerusalem were in Chicago and speculation that the beast in the Book of Revelation was actually a gigantic computer in Brussels. A preacher proclaimed that 1972 would be the last U.S. presidential election as we know it, so I called up my father and told him with complete confidence this prediction would come true. Another man, someone I respected highly, announced that Henry Kissinger was the antichrist. So my friends and I warned people, saying, "Watch that Henry Kissinger. He's got the mark of the beast." A few years later, though, Mr. Kissinger got married. According to our interpretation of Scripture, that took him out of the running.

Before I started Bible college I made a trip to Israel, since the preaching I was hearing placed that nation at the center of God's attention. It so happened that our American tour guide was a self-proclaimed Bible scholar. He had studied Hebrew and Greek for several years, he said. I figured I had hit the jackpot. Here was someone who could clear up for me the confusing passages of the Bible. He did not disappoint me. After the tour began, he dropped the bombshell: he had uncovered the antichrist. He even showed slides of him! It was not Henry Kissinger. His "antichrist" was an Arab I'd never seen before, with big black eyes.

A few months later, my maintenance-crew boss at Bible school told me that by 1975 we would be housing United Nations troops on our campus. He had bought an isolated home in one of the northern states and was storing food and supplies there. With generators for electricity in place, he was ready to move up there in a few years—just before the U.N. troops arrived to combat the Communists.

The year 1975 came, and though no U.N. soldiers had landed, the atmosphere was still charged with excitement over the Second Coming. By then I had completed Bible college and had been hired as youth pastor for a church. The pastor's wife recounted a dream she'd had in which an airborne banner appeared with these words: "Maranatha '75." She thought it meant the rapture would happen by year's end. A prominent Christian television program added credence to her claim by speculating that Jesus would return when the planets lined up in 1982. People who figured on a seven-year tribulation period preceding this celestial phenomenon predicted the rapture would occur in 1975.

Since I was working with college students, I was encouraged to take out a big ad in the campus paper to announce that Jesus was returning in 1975. When I refused, saying, "Well, we might be wrong," I received suspicious looks, and some even questioned my confidence in the Bible. The pastor, convinced that the final day was nearing, wrote a letter to his son letting him know where he would leave the car keys and his insurance policy. Another man in the church announced to his colleagues at work that after the weekend he would not be back.

Such activities may sound extreme, but the people who had interpreted the vision of "Maranatha '75" loved God and led upright lives. I had great respect for them, and I wanted to believe what they said.

We, of course, were not the only ones who made predictions and then had to pick up the pieces when they didn't come to pass. Perhaps the commentator who reached more people than anyone with this message of Christ's imminent return was Hal Lindsey. His book *The Late Great Planet Earth* sold more than eighteen million copies worldwide after its release in 1970, making it the best-selling nonfiction book of the decade. In it Lindsey gave an intricate analysis of current events, which he linked to the fulfillment of prophecies concerning the return of Christ. Lindsey described a chain of cataclysmic events leading to a world war involving a Russian confederacy, an Oriental army of 200 million men, a revived Roman Empire aligned with the United States, and a combined force of Arab and African armies. "Time is short," he told his readers.[3]

Lindsey followed *The Late Great Planet Earth* with a string of best-sellers amplifying his message that world destruction was at hand. Each report of another famine, earthquake, or volcanic eruption added another piece of evidence. Shifting weather patterns signaled the beginning of the end. Each economic downturn previewed a global economic collapse. Lindsey saw superpower tension and Middle Eastern conflict as smoldering tinder ready to explode any day into the conflagration of Armageddon.

David Wilkerson was another voice echoing the message that the world was on the verge of annihilation. His book *The Vision* was promoted as a "terrifying prophecy of Doomsday that is starting to happen now." Published in 1974, it painted a scene of how a rapid and catastrophic breakdown, exacerbated by natural disasters, would beset world civilization beginning in the next decade.

> American food reserves will dwindle—partially due to drought and floods in this country. Wheat, rice, and soybean reserves will be completely exhausted. The demand for corn, rice, and wheat will not be met.[4]

> Floods, hurricanes, tornadoes, and hailstorms will occur more frequently. More than one-third of the United States will be designated a disaster area within the next few years.[5]

> The drastic weather changes that are coming in the next decade will bring with them violent hailstorms of unbelievable proportions.[6]

The same year Wilkerson's book came out, Willard Cantelon wrote *The Day the Dollar Dies*, telling of a coming world government with a new monetary system that would not use hard currency. This author said that numbers would be tattooed on people's foreheads, like the mark of the beast described in Revelation 13, and that people would be unable to buy or sell anything without it. Cantelon said that this was being made possible by a U.S. government computer system "that soon would have complete mastery of man's privacy and control of his every action."[7]

These books were part of a swirl of activity during the late sixties and early seventies that kept the rapture and the return of Christ in the forefront of people's minds. A movie titled *Thief in the Night* portrayed someone who was left behind during the rapture. And Larry Norman's song, "I Wish We'd All Been Ready," rocketed to popularity. One stanza went like this:

> *Man and wife asleep in bed,*
> *She hears a noise and turns her head, he's gone.*
> *I wish we'd all been ready.*
> *Two men coming up a hill,*
> *One disappears and one's left standing still.*
> *I wish we'd all been ready.*
>
> *There's no time to change your mind,*
> *The Son is come and you've been left behind.*[8]

Being "left behind" was a frightening thought. One afternoon, having walked home from a class at Bible college, I went inside our mobile home and was surprised to find that my wife wasn't there. Everything was very still—too still. A horrible thought assaulted me: "I missed the rapture!" I know I'm not the only believer who had an experience like that.

While the fervor has quieted a bit, it periodically picks up again. In 1988, another author pieced together his predictions and named a three-day period in September of that year as the target date for the rapture. Like every prediction before, the days came and went like normal. The author's response was simply to set another date for the Second Coming.

Red-faced results

So what happened as a result of all these bold predictions about the Second Coming? Well, we were left with a lot of red-faced preachers having to stand before their congregations and communities to explain why the predictions did not come to pass. Some of those preachers did some fancy theological footwork to save face. Others didn't bother trying to explain away the failure, and admitted that they missed it. Many have continued to cling to their cause, revising dates and pushing back predictions, insisting on proclaiming impending doom for the world and failure for the church.

After the 1975 rapture date passed uneventfully, I found myself having to pick up the pieces with a group of young, bewildered believers. The members of our college fellowship group had embraced the predictions presented to them. I sat in my office day after day, swamped with counseling appointments, trying to help one after another sort out the event that never was.

Be ye healed

In the midst of the enthusiasm over the Second Coming, there were also several well-known preachers promoting an exciting message of faith and power. In my Bible college years I was eager to absorb everything that touched on this subject.

A classmate and I used to talk on campus about faith and miracles. Late one night he phoned to tell me of an evangelist he was reading about. The man had called for an earthquake to shake up some people who weren't paying attention to what he was saying. Sure enough, the book reported, the ground began to tremble. That kind of authority excited us.

Another Bible college friend, a fellow named Henry, had become a Christian while in Peru searching for a yoga colony. This man had also tried, and abandoned, a number of causes. With hair down to his waist, he had become a fructarian: he not only refused to eat meat in those days, he would not even eat vegetables. Just fruit. This former fructarian wore wire-rimmed glasses with lenses as thick as the bottom of a Coke bottle. Embracing the power and miracles message, we believed God would heal everyone who had faith, including Henry, and we had the Bible verses to back it up.

Yes, the glasses had to go. One night at church he took them off, threw them on the floor, and stomped on them. They were hard to break because they were so thick. Nevertheless he ground the glass into the carpet and put those spectacles out of service. We waited to see what would happen. And we waited. Unfortunately, while we waited Henry was blind as a bat. Weeks after the specs-stomping incident, he would pass me on campus and say, "Is that you, Joe?" For the rest of the term he could barely read the chalkboard in class, even when he sat on the front row. We did witness a miracle, though: Henry drove his '58 Chevy around town all semester and never did hit a single pedestrian.

Henry's bifocals weren't the only casualty of my "superfaith" campaign. At one point I criticized the Bible college president for having a school for deaf people. With all my discernment and sensitivity, I proclaimed to him that the deaf school was an abomination to God and that we should heal the deaf, not teach them to talk with their hands. I prayed for one of the deaf students, assuring him that since I had fasted and prayed about it he would be healed. Though I stuck my fingers deep into his ears and shook him vigorously, I did not deliver the miracle I had promised. The only conclusion my theology allowed was that he lacked the faith to be healed.

Enthusiastically, I embraced the faith cause. The problem was, I did not see the results that were supposed to be produced. This troubled me and started stirring up more than a few questions. Finally, I had to get some answers.

The opportunity arose to see firsthand the ministry of a key leader in the faith movement. Reports were that many people had been miraculously healed through this man's ministry. An evening service was scheduled at a church about 200 miles from campus. I drove down to see for myself, arriving a few minutes before the service began. People with all kinds of ailments were there. They were obviously hopeful that this healing service would dramatically change their lives. I noticed some children who had come in brand-new clothes, anticipating their first step out of a wheelchair. The preaching was powerful. I believed every word. The minister concluded with a prayer for healing. Everyone was healed, he said, "from the crown of your head to the soles of your feet." But, of the dozens there in wheelchairs, not one stood up. After the meeting I went down toward the platform, where I saw mothers crying as they wheeled their disappointed children away.

Unfortunately, I felt that I was getting some of my answers. I could no longer espouse with confidence the theory that healings were automatic, stimulated almost mechanically by words about faith. My frustration forced me to admit a discouraging fact about myself as well as about the superfaith preachers I was imitating: we were making promises we could not keep.

Did our lack of success mean that miracles could not happen today, that signs and wonders only took place in the first century? I knew that was not true. It did not even occur to me as a possibility. I had already seen too many Scripture-fulfilling incidents to seriously consider that position.

In the midst of my confusion I was asked to speak at a youth meeting at a movie theater in St. Louis. Sitting among the high school students were an older lady with white hair and an elderly gentleman in a dark blue suit. They came to the front afterward, wanting me to pray for them. Curiosity overtook me. "I don't want to be rude," I said, "but can I ask you a question? What in the world are you doing here?"

He said they were hungry to experience more of God, and he proceeded to explain why, telling a most remarkable story. His wife had been disabled for thirty-seven years with a degenerative spinal disease. Her life consisted of constant pain and frequent hospital stays. Friends encouraged them to attend a Kathryn Kuhlman meeting at Kiel Auditorium in St. Louis; and, though not of the doctrinal persuasion that God performs miracles of healing today, they went to the meeting. Midway through the service Miss Kuhlman paused. She said there was a woman present, sitting somewhere in the middle section toward the front, who had had a spinal condition for thirty-seven years. God was healing her right then, she said. At that instant, this man told me, his wife was healed. Tears welled up in his eyes as he shared the story with me. To accentuate her husband's account, the woman bent over and touched her toes.

The Kathryn Kuhlman encounter

Not long after that meeting in St. Louis, Kathryn Kuhlman came to our city and had a meeting at the church where I worked as custodian. We needed every available person for ushering, so I was recruited. While I was helping people find their seats, I heard someone call my name. It was the pastor.

"Joe, I have to go out and start the meeting. Wait here for Miss Kuhlman. When she comes out of my office, escort her onto the platform."

Looking through the window in his office, I saw this lady with her hands up in the air, pacing from one side of his office to the other. She spotted me standing about twenty-five feet away, gave a big wave, and started walking toward me. When she came and stood in front of me, all my questions about faith, formulas, and believing God for miracles came to the surface. But I couldn't say anything.

Puzzled, I looked at this woman who was old enough to be my grandmother. She wore bright red lipstick extending well above her lip line and was dressed in a long flowing gown. Some thoughts started crossing my mind, not very flattering ones. I was aware that there were many people in the auditorium who were skeptical about her methods as well as her message; others were hurting, desperate for help. And in front of me stood this elderly lady. I wondered what would come of it all. I looked Miss Kuhlman in the eye and asked, "Are you ready?"

She not only heard my words but also read my expression of skepticism. She recognized my bewilderment, my questions, my doubts. "I'm sorry," I said immediately, slapping myself in the face for my foolish question. She reared her head back and laughed. Then she lunged forward, grabbed my face, and drew it right up next to hers.

"*I don't know,*" she whispered. "*I don't know. We're just going to believe God. Let's just see what He's going to do.*"

Aware, somehow, of the Holy Spirit's touch, I started to cry. She laughed again, grabbed my face the same as before, and as if for emphasis repeated her plan. "*I just don't know. I don't know why. I don't know how. But let's just believe God.*"

By this time, my knees were shaking, my face was flushed, and I felt like a piece of wilted lettuce. Stumbling back against the wall, I actually felt the presence of God. I didn't know what to say. I couldn't move. She grabbed me once again. My strength was gone, my heart exposed; and God, once and for all, planted a seed in my spirit that I cherish to this day: "*Let's just believe God and see what He is going to do.*"

Miss Kuhlman talked to me for a few minutes about my life. Then she glanced up toward the auditorium. "Are we going to have a meeting today or not?" she asked. Pulling myself together, I escorted her, as best I could under the circumstances, to the platform. Actually, I was so weak by then that she did more escorting than I did.

I was a changed person. One touch from Jesus, through that single encounter with a woman of God, had instantly stilled the storm in my heart. God used an elderly woman from Concordia, Missouri, without even a high school education, to blast away the arrogance of a young Bible college student who thought he could figure out some formula to manipulate God.

When I joined my wife in the audience, she looked at me and immediately asked, "What happened to you?" I could not answer. For the rest of that service I watched in awe as people were dramatically healed from serious medical conditions. For the first time, though, I knew I was watching God do what He wanted to do, rather than hearing someone issue Him instructions.

Ever since then, I have never questioned the fact that God indeed performs miracles, some quite dramatic at that. But I also became convinced about something else: I do not really understand how He does it; I do not always know when He wants to do it; and I'm not so sure I understand that much about why He does it. And, I have to admit, I am a bit skeptical about those who claim they do.

Holier than thou

A third cause that caught my fancy had to do with striving for personal perfection. My friends and I were trying, through discipline and self-inflicted rules, to achieve a level of righteousness that really can only come from God's work in our hearts. Because we focused on the outward appearance of spirituality, we ended up setting a rigid code of Christian behavior to which we tried to hold ourselves, as well as everyone else. I saw this zeal for perfect performance as a way of rejecting the mediocrity of the church and being radical for Jesus, but it was just an exercise in futility.

One time I thought it would be good to spend several days fasting and praying. I tried to stay awake all night and really give the effort my all. I had read about the famous Welsh Revival, in which a pastor emerged from his study with his countenance so aglow that people couldn't even look at him. I expected to follow suit and step out of the prayer chapel with a face like Moses', shining with the presence of God.

It didn't work out quite that way, though. Instead of getting a spiritual surge, I became hungry and irritable. When I ended my fast, my wife didn't sense that I had met with the Master. The first thing she said was that I needed a shave.

The pursuit of perfection soon slips into a competitive kind of Christianity in which people compare their performance with each other's. Subconsciously, we put together a complete package of what we feel is the correct Christian lifestyle. In the case of my Bible-school friends and me, the result was a self-righteous disapproval of anyone we thought did not meet our spiritual standards. Some of us, for instance, were questioning the commitment of Christians who bought new cars, rather than driving used cars and putting the savings in the offering plate.

Zeal and holiness are vital characteristics for productive

Christians. But if zeal produces self-righteous radicals who criticize all who fall short of their religious standards, something has gone awry. Instead of true holiness, we produce legalism. It's remarkable how this attitude can take root in the hearts of genuine believers who want to please God. My wife, Dawn, worked with a girl in California who was convinced she was closer to God and a better Christian than Dawn. Why? Because Dawn wore make-up and she did not.

When our fellowship started in the mid-seventies, we were a casual bunch. In our Friday night services we led worship with guitars, and nobody wore a coat and tie. I had an interesting chat with a pastor's wife who strongly objected to our style.

"So, you think you're really seeing people get saved at those rock concerts on Friday night?" she asked, clearly skeptical.

"Well, we're going along the best we can," I said. Actually, many young men and women were committing themselves to serving God. (Some of them are now the elders, deacons, and home group leaders in our church).

"What these young people need is a preacher," she said.

"I'm doing the best I can," I replied.

"I mean a *real* preacher," she said.

As we talked I invited her to come preach. She declined, saying she had a youth group of her own, and she assured me that our young women who were wearing men's shirts definitely would not make the rapture.

The results

I want to be careful here not to oversimplify and totally disregard all the teachings described above, which, for the most part, were promoted by sincere preachers of the gospel. Of course, each of these emphases is lined with elements of truth. It's a fact that Jesus will come again and that we should be prepared for His return; that God is powerful and performs miracles; and that God has called us to walk in holiness and righteousness. But at the same time we must face another fact: the fruit of these teachings has not been all that good. Some of it, frankly, has been tragic.

Nothing makes Christians look more ridiculous than predicting specific dates for the rapture, the tribulation, the antichrist's appearance, and the Second Coming, only to see the dates come and go and be replaced by more dates further ahead on the calendar. Let's face it—it's embarrassing.

The pat theories of the faith preachers turned out to be more talk than substance. Not only were scores of hopeful believers left in their various conditions, but even more tragically, some have died in valiant attempts to put faith formulas into practice. People have thrown away their medicine, believing that God would heal them without it. Such practices have cost some their lives. For others who have become cynical and bitter, it has cost them their faith.

What began as a radical commitment to personal holiness turned into an ugly form of legalism marked by competitiveness and judgments based on outward performance. Believers were pitted against one another in a struggle to win the righteousness trophy.

In short, I found that the various teachings I had latched onto produced embarrassment and frustration, confusion and competition, pride and pain—not exactly the goals of successful Christian living.

CHAPTER 2

THE PRODUCT

There is a simple way to evaluate various teachings that gain popularity on the Christian landscape, and you don't have to be a theologian. The best test is to ask, "What are the results?" Or, in biblical language, "What kind of fruit does this teaching bear?"[1]

I did not see good fruit produced when the teachings I adopted early in my Christian life took center stage. In short, when put to the test of daily living, they didn't work.

Hold the hype

Speaking to a national gathering of church leaders in 1986, Bob Mumford struck a sympathetic chord with many when he spoke of the rising tide of "hype" in contemporary Christianity. In effect, he said we've had all we can take:

> Perhaps you received the same letter I did. On the envelope was a bold announcement: "You have just won $10 million."
>
> I looked it over. Then I did the same thing everyone else did with it. I flicked it in the circular file—under "T" for trash. Why? I knew the people with all the big promises wouldn't deliver.

Those ridiculous gimmicks just don't capture my imagination anymore. There's an interesting law at work in the marketplace: the law of diminishing returns. We've heard all the pitches. We know all the gimmicks. Americans cannot be hyped anymore. After years of promises without product we are, as they say in the business world, "glossing ourselves out of the market." We need to move into the product phase. We've got to quit promising and start producing.

The church is running out of superlatives. After spectacular, where do you go? After so much hype, one more turn of the screw and the thread is stripped.

We need to discriminate between what's genuine and what's not. I went to Jamaica and kept hearing of the thousands and thousands of people converted in a revival there. I did a little research and discovered that, according to the figures I was hearing, more people were saved in Jamaica than ever lived in Jamaica. There was only one way to interpret that: the same people were getting saved night after night.

Right now, Americans are short on product. A man I know bought a brand new American-made automobile. It was barely out of the showroom when he tried to shut the glove compartment door. It fell off in his hand. I drive a Japanese-made Honda. Why? It works.[2]

It's not hard to get on television or travel from meeting to meeting and make all kinds of claims and promises. But our generation has been duped a few too many times by people whose lives do not back up the message they preach. People no longer swallow everything that comes their way just because it's said with a sincere smile. They want to know what goes on behind the scenes, what happens when the cameras stop rolling and the stagehands flick off the floodlights.

"You say this message will work?" they reply. "Okay, prove it. Let's see some evidence." As they say in Missouri, "Show me."

Show me

That's fair enough. I have heard a lot of talk on my journey through the maze of Christian causes, and I've discovered that not everything is as it seems to be. I bought into some of those showroom promises, only to get down the road a few miles and find that my shiny new purchase was clanking and sputtering. So I started paying less attention to the pitch and more attention to the product.

I'll be honest: this book has a pitch; it attempts to persuade, as most books do. But I'm going to do my best to hold the hype and make a straightforward case based on the evidence that I have assembled. I've got confidence that this "product" works because I've been testing it myself for almost fifteen years. And I know several hundred other people who have invested their lives in the same product; later some of them will explain in their own words how it has worked for them. What product am I talking about? It's the local church.

That term—local church—may be enough to lead some to put this book down. The church is hardly a subject that arouses their interest, let alone fills them with excitement or heartfelt passion. Even the word *church* seems to many to be tarnished and grimy. For others, it means something boring, lifeless, and irrelevant. But I ask that you set aside any preconceived ideas of what *church* is all about, because this book presents a different product from what most people think of as a church. I'm not talking about an echoing dungeon or a religious version of the "Ted Mack Amateur Hour." I'm talking about a purpose of enormous significance, one so important that groups of people will set aside their individual dreams to turn this vision into reality in their communities.

Our church began with a few people who believed that the message of the Bible is to love God and to commit yourself to people as the evidence of that love. We believed that giving ourselves to this message would produce a product that could stand close examination and be proven genuine.

I am not trying to hold up our church as a perfect model, because it isn't. Like every other group of believers, we are full of flaws, and we depend on God's grace every step of the way. We have made mistakes, taken some wrong turns, and fully expect that God will keep making corrections in our course. But I have included information about this church simply because it's the "laboratory" I've been laboring in for most of my adult life. It's the "product" I can describe to show you the concepts I want to communicate.

This church is by no means the only group of believers finding satisfaction in a lifestyle that works. More and more churches are emerging, in the United States and across the world, that are responding to a new emphasis on the church.[3] Our congregation is one which is given wholeheartedly to the single vision of building God's church. This has become the central cause of our lives.

Blue jeans and T-shirts

Our story begins in the early 1970s, when the "Jesus Movement" was gathering droves of young people during the fading days of the hippie era. Young people like me had been betrayed by promises of a bright new world on the horizon. They had believed the message about love and freedom, but had instead experienced pain, turmoil, and bondage. Now they were grasping for truth, for God.

In the Midwest, dozens of students in Columbia, Missouri, a university town of about 60,000, had been drawn into a relationship with the central figure of human history. They had encountered Jesus Christ. He had forgiven them and shown them His kindness, and they felt a great debt of gratitude. Their common desire was simply "to know God."

These young people began meeting in our home on Friday nights. We studied the Bible, worshiped, prayed, talked, and just "hung out" together. Word spread, and more people kept coming until they filled the couches and chairs and spilled out into the hallways. People came in blue jeans and T-shirts, tennis shoes and sandals. Clothes were not an issue for us; what people looked like was irrelevant. We just wanted to follow Jesus, and casual was the only style we knew.

I still recall our first "offering." It occurred to someone that there would not be any popcorn and raisins to snack on the following Friday unless we all chipped in. So someone passed a battered, gray felt hat. After that, the hat's owner, Bob, made sure that it made the rounds each week. He became and still is the church treasurer. In a few years, instead of quarters and dimes, he would be handling hundreds of thousands of dollars.

Unfamiliar territory

We set our course in a direction that seemed to us to lead through uncharted waters; we felt like Christopher Columbus setting out for the New World. Much of the "old world" had to be left behind. For some of us, the old world consisted of fruitless religious systems and traditions. For others, it involved careers, ambitions, and dreams that would have steered them away from the direction in which we wanted to go as a church. Though we were excited about embarking on this venture together, our crew of unconventional explorers was not exactly the envy of every church. Nor were most of our friends and family members excited about our departure from the old world. We learned right from the beginning that there is a price to pay for pioneering.

Though we were heading into unfamiliar territory, we had a clear destination in mind. It had to do with a picture we saw in the Bible.

CHAPTER 3

THE JIGSAW PUZZLE

Imagine a businessman who has been cruising through his day-to-day life at breakneck speed. Finally, relaxing at home in his easy chair, he tries to think of something restful to do, something that could provide a little relief from the everyday madness. Suddenly, he remembers—jigsaw puzzles! Remembering the satisfaction they used to bring, he pulls on his jacket, lifts the car keys out of his pocket, and slips out the door.

The missing box

"Aisle 24, across from the teddy bears," the clerk says, answering the man's question about where to find the jigsaw puzzles. He passes the plumbing supplies and the house paint. Just beyond the greeting cards, he turns to his left, down aisle 24. "Something is wrong here," he says to himself. Aisle 24 is lined with several large unmarked brown bins, each filled with hundreds of puzzle pieces. Perplexed, the man turns away to find a clerk.

"Sir, I came to pick up a jigsaw puzzle, and all I found were these bins full of loose pieces," he says.

"That's why they're on sale," the clerk replies. "Which bin would you like?"

"Well, I don't know. How do I know what the puzzle is supposed to look like?"

"You don't. You'll just have to do the best you can."

"Where are the boxes?" the shopper asks, making one last effort to make sense out of this confusion. "The box the pieces come in, with the picture on it. I need the picture. How else will I know whether I want to buy the puzzle?"

"I'm sorry, sir," the clerk says. "The boxes were all damaged in shipping. All the pieces are there in the bins. But there's no box. No picture."

The puzzle seeker is exasperated by now. He came looking for relief from the hectic world around him. Instead he is only finding more frustration, more chaos. Still, he picks up a bin; then, even more tense than when he got off work, he stomps toward the checkout counter.

When he gets home, he dumps the hundreds of colorful shapes on the kitchen table.

"What's this puzzle going to look like?" his wife says.

"I don't know. There's no box. No picture. The clerk said just to do the best I can."

The big picture

Now imagine a new believer, hungry to learn about the Lord and eager to dig into the Bible. Instead of giving him clear instructions, though, a friend hands him a big bin full of pieces of paper. The friend spent several days taking the thousand-plus pages of a Bible, all sixty-six books, carefully cutting out each verse and placing the separate scriptures in the bin.

"All the truth is there," he assures the new convert. "Good luck figuring it out."

As the new believer filters through the verses, he comes upon little pieces of truth—everything from God's dealings with Adam and Eve to the streets of gold described in Revelation. But he has absolutely no idea how it all fits together.

That is basically the way it is for most of us when we begin our Christian lives. We do not start out with the picture on the puzzle box, which would give us a clear idea of our goal. Rather, we find ourselves surrounded by bits of truth, confused about how they all fit together and what they all mean.

My question is this: Do we have to remain baffled about the key theme of the Bible, or is there a way to find out what the picture on the Bible's puzzle box looks like? Are we doomed to a life of confusion, never knowing what God wants to accomplish on earth? Is the picture just a matter of opinion? I think not.

The search continues

These were the questions I began wrestling with after I had experienced enough disappointment to know that every teaching would not necessarily pan out. I wasn't interested anymore in jumping from one teaching emphasis to another. I yearned for a picture that would not leave me disappointed. In my efforts during my Bible college days to determine what that picture might be, I studied the Bible; but I had to end up admitting, "I don't understand this." I could answer the questions on the test and memorize passages of Scripture, but I did not know what it all meant.

I was being taught how to preach from a pulpit; administer a Christian education program; preside over baptisms, weddings, and funerals; and conduct a church business meeting. But my most desperate need was to know the message that would unlock the Bible. I wanted to see the picture that God had painted—the picture that's on the puzzle box. I wanted to understand what the finished product was supposed to look like. Without that, I knew we would all be left scrambling after stray pieces of truth, trying unsuccessfully to make something work. That would have been too frustrating for me.

In the Bible I found someone I could identify with, someone equally frustrated with the confusion of his day.

Story of a seeker

While Jesus was on the earth He fielded many questions, especially from the religious leaders of His day. As you would expect, He was good at reading the intent of the questioners, and He responded accordingly.

Luke 20 records a confrontation between Jesus and some Pharisees, Sadducees, and scribes. They try to corner Jesus with questions about His authority, to which He responds with a question of His own, one that puts them in a quandary. Realizing they are trapped, they stand in embarrassed silence.

Jesus uses this golden opportunity to launch into a parable about the wicked tenants of a vineyard owner. His story recounts the pattern in which time and again the people of Israel have rejected the prophets sent to them to explain God's message. The priests and scholars, who have remained to listen, are a little slow to catch on. Finally, though, they realize that Jesus is talking about them. Red-faced with rage, they stomp out and start looking for some way to quiet Jesus for good.

You would think that these men would have had enough by now, but apparently not. A little later they send back some of their brethren to start up the argument all over again. This time the religious notables take a different tack. They badger the Master with hypocritical questions about taxes and marriage in heaven, trying to trip Him up. One scribe, however, sits silently through the entire exchange, listening intently. He hears Jesus tell of how this succession of messengers sent by the Father all met the same fate—death. This scribe, a custodian of the Scriptures, knows the Old Testament well and recognizes what Jesus is saying. Those of the past who had been in his position had missed the message and mistreated the messenger.

As the scribe observes his colleagues busily badmouthing the carpenter from Nazareth, perhaps he ponders the impact Jesus seems to have. People come to Him sick, and He heals them. People who are ignorant of the Law, poor, and deeply entrenched in sin are dramatically changed when they come to Him. These people are so thrilled that they are causing an uproar all across Israel.

Then, perhaps, the scribe questions his own effectiveness. "What happens," he muses, "when people come to me and my colleagues for help? They hear of many rules. We recite our interpretation of the teachings of Moses, the history of Israel, and the list of unclean foods. We give information and demand obedience—but people remain unchanged."

What's most important?

The scribe hears Jesus conveying more than regulations and religious practices. When the sharp exchanges between his colleagues and Jesus subside, he seizes his opportunity to find out what Jesus believes is most important to God. "What commandment is the foremost of all?" he asks.

Jesus knows that, unlike the rest, this man is genuinely looking for an answer to the key question of life: What does God want from me? Where do I fit into this picture? This leader of the people no longer found meaning in the things being preached around him. He believed in the God of Abraham, Isaac, and Jacob; but he wasn't sure he really knew Him that well, and he needed confirmation of his understanding of God's message to His people. He was asking Jesus to help him put everything together.

Jesus doesn't answer the man as He has other religious leaders. For this seeker, He puts His brush to the canvas and with a few strokes outlines His picture plainly:

> The most important [commandment] is this: . . . "Love the Lord your God with all your heart and with all your soul and with all your mind and with all your strength." The second is this: "Love your neighbor as yourself." There is no commandment greater than these.[1]

Jesus' words rang true in the man's heart. He immediately demonstrated to Jesus that he grasped the difference between the picture Jesus was painting and the one fashioned by him and his colleagues. He said:

To love [God] with all your heart, with all your understanding and with all your strength, and to love your neighbor as yourself is more important than all burnt offerings and sacrifices.[2]

In front of all his peers, the scribe was conceding, "Teacher, you're right. All these pieces of the puzzle, the pieces we emphasize—sacrifices and burnt offerings and all they represent—mean nothing unless they are somehow connected with loving God and loving your neighbor."

Jesus gave him the greatest commandment. He gave him the foundation upon which he could build everything else in his life. And it made sense—perfect sense. Jesus had painted the picture that is on the puzzle box. To assemble pieces of truth according to any other picture would only mean more confusion, more failure.

At the conclusion of their conversation, Jesus commended the scribe, as He had few other religious leaders:

"You're not far from the kingdom."

A sensible picture

This story may seem simple enough, but its implications are enormous. The scribe had absorbed the foundational truth of the Bible, a truth that our generation may have exchanged for other more stimulating, but less sensible, teachings.

Like the scribe, if we are going to set a new course for our lives, we will have to be confident that we have found the right answer to the key question: What is the ultimate purpose of God? What is that one unifying force behind the hundreds of truths of the Bible, that one theme that ties everything together? What is God determined to accomplish? What has been His primary objective throughout history? The answer to these questions will give us the picture on the puzzle box.

David Matthew, an English pastor and author, poses the question about God's ultimate purpose in his book, *Church*

Adrift. He helps clarify the picture by distinguishing between the many good things that God desires and His ultimate goal.

> Within any grand purpose there are always lesser purposes which contribute toward the greater one. Suppose a man plans to sail the Atlantic single-handed in his own boat. That is his grand purpose. Not having any previous experience of boat-building, he enrolls in a one-year course of evening classes to learn the basics. He now has a subsidiary purpose—to see the course through and then to build his boat. But what's the good of having a boat if he can't sail it? So the next subsidiary purpose is to learn sailing under an expert, involving regular trips to the coast on weekends.
>
> While this is going on, he spends his evenings on yet another secondary project—learning the principles of navigation from library books. Then he signs himself up for a year-long program of offshore races in order to gain experience. In the meantime he must raise the cash for his Atlantic crossing, seeking sponsorship and turning his own investments into capital. Each of these secondary projects, however, is just one aspect of that one, overriding purpose that motivates them all—a single-handed crossing of the Atlantic in his own boat.
>
> It's because God's grand purpose is like this that different Christians give different answers when asked what it is. In a sense, they are all true. Typical answers might be:
> • The evangelization of the world
> • To have a people who gladly bow the knee to Christ
> • The defeat of Satan
> • To deal with sin in human society
> • The universal rule of Jesus Christ
> • To bring justice and peace
> • To make us like Jesus

•To take us to heaven
•The restoration of all things

There are others we could add to the list, all equally valid. But we need somehow to rise above all these sub-sections and ask ourselves what is God's ultimate purpose. What is *the* grand, overall design that gives meaning to all the rest? What, in other words, is the divine equivalent of that transatlantic crossing?[3]

If you have known disappointment as a Christian, or if you feel you have yet to experience the full satisfaction of a lifestyle that works, this is the first question for you to address: What is it that, above all, God wants? I think it's fair to assume that this picture you seek is not abstract. If the picture on the box were a painting consisting of globs of color slapped randomly onto a canvas, we would not be able to have the same understanding of what it meant. Each one looking at the pieces would draw his own conclusion. But rather than toss out a confusing jumble of pieces, the Bible presents a clear picture of God's purpose for His people, a picture unmuddied by the ever-shifting opinions of men.

Environmental influence

A word of caution: To accept the Bible's teaching on God's ultimate purpose, you will need to part with any conflicting ideas you may have absorbed from the influences around you. Like the scribe who had to look beyond the viewpoints of his colleagues, you may discover truths that will propel you into remarkably different theological terrain.

Recognize that your current view of the painting on the puzzle box will be colored by what others around you see. New believers tend to adopt the picture painted by more seasoned believers around them. When a person is born again, he becomes a baby all over again. He begins learning how to walk and how to talk in his new spiritual life. Children don't have to try particularly hard to learn their parents' language or to mimic their accent. It comes naturally to them. They do not realize that they are only imitating their parents when they speak English, or French, or Spanish, but they are.

Spiritually speaking, we also tend to repeat what we are taught. Though we like to think of ourselves as independent thinkers, our views are shaped to a large degree by those believers who have imparted to us a way of thinking about the Bible.

I absorbed others' views of the Bible in my early Christian years, views that I eventually began to question. Something began to happen in my heart: I became less satisfied with the picture that had been painted for me, less convinced that it was the right one. Ultimately, that picture began to fade. I wanted God to show me the picture He had in His heart—not one that merely highlighted certain pieces of the puzzle, but the one that properly combined all the pieces.

SECTION TWO:

THE PICTURE

CHAPTER 4

GOD WANTS
A FAMILY

An image began taking shape for me. It was an artistic masterpiece of colors and shapes. As I got a closer look, the shapes I saw outlined were those of people, all kinds of people caring for one another, serving one another, preferring one another. Looking over this sea of humanity is God Himself, pleased to see His creation honoring Him by pouring out their lives for each other.

These multitudes have a name for their God; they call Him "Father." And God has a name for them: "My children." The picture that identifies God's ultimate goal is a picture of a family.

David Matthew described the end that God is pursuing:

> God's great purpose is simply *to have a family—a very large one!* He's looking for sons who will love him and obey him gladly and freely.
>
> You think that sounds a bit flat and disappointing? Maybe you thought the "family" picture was just another way of describing to finite creatures like ourselves the mysterious relationship of the infinite God with his people. No, it's the other way around entirely. Fatherhood starts with God, not with men. He is "the Father from whom every family in heaven and on earth derives its name."[1] Human fatherhood and

human families are mini-versions, tiny replicas of the
wonderful fatherhood of God and his great family of
redeemed people. And fatherhood and family are at
the very heart of God's eternal purpose.[2]

Hunger for relationships

Evidence is overwhelming that the deepest desire of the human
heart is for relationships. Each of us has an innate desire to be
loved, and our deepest fulfillment comes from giving love. Most
psychologists, sociologists, and other secular observers, as well
as theologians, concur with that premise. Why? Is there something
about the way God made us that brings us to that conclusion?
I think so. The Bible says that when God made us, He placed
eternity in our hearts.[3] What does that mean?

My little boy gave me an example of the nature of the eternity
God has built into his heart. When he was nine months old, not
even walking yet, he received a visit from a fourteen-month-old.
When my son saw his visitor, his legs and arms started flying, and
a big smile swept across his face. Immediately he crawled
toward his new friend. He was obviously too young to have been
taught the art of formal introductions, so his response was
completely natural. That innate desire for relationships comes
from the "eternity" in his heart. When he gets older, though, he
will temper that enthusiasm and learn how to act as though he
could live alone, independently of others—just like the rest of
us.

People not only have an innate need for relationships; God
has also planted in us a compelling desire for permanency in
those relationships—another facet of the eternity He has set in
our hearts. I saw this very human feeling demonstrated at a
funeral, where I observed a woman who was burying her
husband after more than thirty years of marriage. When we were
walking away from the grave site, she didn't want to leave. She
let out a shriek, crying, "No! No!" Something inside her rebelled
when death broke off a relationship that she knew should have
continued.

Anyone who has had part of his heart torn out by the loss of a close friend or family member knows the pain of a broken relationship. We try to overcome our feelings and comfort each other, but something inside us says, "This ought not to be."

At any cost

It's easy to illustrate how the concepts of relationship and eternity are connected. Several years ago I spoke to a group of high school students on the subject of hell.

"Who would be afraid to go to hell?" I asked them. Few responded.

"How many of you believe that you're on your way to hell?" Several indicated they did—and that they weren't afraid to go. When I asked why they thought it wouldn't be that bad, one said:

"Because I'll be with my friends."

They all nodded in agreement, with complete sincerity. I asked them if they were serious; they assured me they were. This was no joke.

This group issued a strong testimony to their need for relationships. These young people were willing to endure the ultimate penalty for the sake of maintaining their friendships, not realizing, of course, that in hell there is no such thing as friendship. Even this foolish response to my question, though, demonstrates the human longing for an eternal relationship.

Universal agreement

The centrality of our need for relationship is evident in the signs of our culture: its art, its literature, its music. You need only to punch a few buttons on your car radio to tune into pop culture's fascination with relationships. Whether it's country-western, new age, or rock and roll, the lyrics inevitably turn to love and affection. Music has a unique way of portraying and stirring emotions that we all experience in relationships, from the wonder and delight of a new friendship to the hurt and loneliness of rejection.

It's ironic that secular entertainers and experts can accurately identify the deepest human need, yet people fall so short in the ability to satisfy it.

A relationship kingdom

Isn't it true that a person's greatest joy and deepest sorrow are rooted in relationships? This need for relationship is the continuing theme of the Bible. Everything contained in it operates within that context. Consider, for example, this scripture:

> Owe no one anything, except to love one another; for he who loves his neighbor has fulfilled the law. The commandments, "You shall not commit adultery, you shall not kill, you shall not steal, you shall not covet," and any other commandment, are summed up in this sentence, "You shall love your neighbor as yourself." Love does no wrong to a neighbor; therefore love is the fulfilling of the law.[4]

The thread of relationship in this scripture holds together the entire Bible. See if you can think of a single event recounted in Scripture, for example a single instruction from one of the epistles, or a single passage in Psalms or Proverbs, that does not ultimately bring us back to the fundamental issue of relationship.

God's work throughout history has been to train us to have proper relationships with Him and with each other. Proper relationships define and distinguish the kingdom of God.

The 'kingdom'

"The kingdom of God" is a key term in the Bible. In fact, Jesus tells us to give this kingdom higher priority than even the basic needs for survival, such as food, clothing, and shelter. "Kingdom of God" is such a lofty phrase, though, that it's hard to nail down exactly what it means. It stirs up vague notions of some realm where God lives and operates—a place far beyond our grasp, like the Land of Oz or some kind of science fiction fantasy. As Christians, we need to understand a little more concretely what this kingdom is all about.

In preparing the manuscript for this book, I asked a woman on an airplane some questions to help me find out what people think about spiritual matters. A successful career woman, she was traveling to Florida on business. I told her I wanted to play a little word-association game. I asked her to listen to words and phrases, then quickly say whatever related words came to mind. Then I rattled off a list of words.

"Bible," I said.

"Confusing," she replied.

"Heaven."

"Harps. Clouds."

"Kingdom of God," I said.

"Mystical. Far away," she replied. Then she asked, "How am I doing?"

"You're answering the way most people I talk to do," I told her. "But when you read the Bible, you find out those answers are wrong."

Her responses echoed the feeling of the majority of people in the baby-boom generation, but these are very different answers from what the Bible gives. None of the words she used to describe the kingdom of God give an indication of something one would seek first above everything else. None of her answers reflect the yearning for relationship that God has put in her heart.

Right relationship

The most concise and straightforward definition of the kingdom of God is found in Paul's epistle to the Romans: "The kingdom of God is not food and drink but righteousness and peace and joy in the Holy Spirit."[5]

An opportunity arose to explain this verse when I spoke as a guest lecturer in a graduate-level counseling class at the University of Missouri, a class composed of people representing a wide variety of cultures and religious viewpoints. My assignment was to explain the spiritual side of man. God has placed in all of us a desire for His kingdom, I told the class. Everyone, I said, instinctively knows that this kingdom is the only solution to the social, political, and economic problems we face. I then stated that when I was finished they all would agree. Everyone perked up at that assertion, and the somewhat skeptical professor thought I had checkmated myself.

To begin my presentation, I wrote on the chalkboard the key words of this passage. I wrote "kingdom of God" at the top, then in a column underneath I wrote the words "righteousness," "peace," and "joy." Opposite each of these words I wrote its meaning: I wrote "right relationships" across from "righteousness," "security" across from "peace," and "expression" across from "joy." Then I began asking questions.

"Is there anyone here whose heart has been broken due to a relationship breakdown?" I asked.

Several responded. One talked about his painful divorce, one mentioned her parents' divorce, and another referred to a betrayal by a friend.

"What happens when a trust is broken?" was my next question. The class mentioned resentment, depression, cynicism, fear, and so on. All agreed that broken relationships lead to insecurity—just the opposite of peace.

At this point some recounted the details of other relationship breakdowns; their faces reflected the emotional scars. Others were even fighting back tears.

"Can joy be genuine if there is an absence of security?" I then asked. The response was unanimous. All the breakdowns in society, the class agreed, could be traced back to relationship.

Once we reached agreement, I announced, "Now we're going to disagree."

"Right relationships among people are impossible because of the disease called 'sin,'" I said. "Sin can be best understood as selfishness, and the only cure has been provided by the king of this kingdom I just described."

I then explained the reason for Jesus' death and resurrection, and the necessity of being in proper relationship with Him. That relationship is the prerequisite for the kingdom of God coming to us.

A woman raised her hand. "Is that what the Bible teaches?" she asked. I said yes. "I went to church all my life, and I've never heard anything like that before," she said. After a minute she raised her hand again. "I want this right now."

"I don't believe this," the professor said. "You're getting converts right in my class."

This woman grasped a new understanding of righteousness. The common perception of this word is shrouded in religious confusion and rooted in a man-made list of rules and regulations that lead us to believe it can be obtained by observing religious exercises.

But righteousness means right relationships, and that can only come by the grace God extended to us in Jesus. Peace, the security that comes from right relationships, becomes the fruit, and joy the outward evidence. This joy is a genuine expression of security, not just a fleeting emotion.

So, how important are relationships? So important that we could rephrase Paul's words to read, "The kingdom of God is relationships." The three aspects he listed—righteousness, peace, and joy—can only be understood in terms of people relating properly to God and to others.

Fathers and sons

Countless expressions used in the Bible denote family-like relationships among the people of God. God is "our Father," and we are His "sons" and "daughters." The body of people who serve God is referred to as the "household" of faith. The Bible says "pure religion" is caring for orphans and widows.[6] Psalms states that God has placed the lonely in families. The Word of

God instructs us to see fellow believers as members of a family, treating older women as mothers, older men as fathers, younger men as brothers, younger women as sisters. Likewise, Jesus said that those who follow Him will receive a hundredfold of mothers, fathers, sisters, and brothers.

All God's instructions are built on the foundation of relationships. The Ten Commandments, for example, all have to do with keeping sound our relationships with God and with other people. When you steal, it damages a relationship. When you lie, it hurts someone. When you commit adultery, someone suffers. When you don't love God with all your heart, mind, soul, and strength, it hinders your relationship with Him.

The legalism threat

Without this understanding of the "relationship" theme of the Bible, the various scriptural instructions on how to live can easily lead to legalism, which is a powerful relationship killer. The root of legalism is failure to understand God's intent. In a legalistic framework, we become like the boy who worked hard to get straight "A's" in school to impress his dad. One night his younger brother, a "C" student, asked for help studying. The older son refused, because taking the time away from his own homework might mean he would get a lower grade. He wanted to please his father, but he didn't realize that getting a "B" for the sake of helping his brother would bring even greater pleasure than a selfishly earned "A." A son who loves his brother brings a father far greater joy than a perfect report card. Sons have trouble seeing that.

It's easy to develop this distorted, legalistic view of what God desires of us. The people in Israel kept getting it wrong; most of them were satisfied in knowing they had kept the rules. That was about the extent of their religion. But when Jesus came, He turned that type of thinking on its head. He made it clear that God's greatest concern is love from a pure heart, not our capacity to read and follow an instruction manual.

The obedience God wants comes from knowing Him. It goes far beyond memorizing a list of His likes and dislikes. Like the son driven to attain perfection, we end up missing the point if obedience becomes the end rather than the means. We drift into legalism when we look at the rules rather than the reason for them, when we focus on our performance rather than on our purpose.

Every thought in the Bible, every doctrine, every teaching has to do with God's desire for relationship with and among His children. Nothing makes sense outside the context of relationships, outside the objective of building a family.

When I first started thinking along these lines, it had a dramatic impact on me. But as I read through the Bible with the relationship principle in mind, some things I had never been able to understand before started making sense to me.

Theological maze

When you look at Christians in the world today, you generally do not see a spirited corps of zealous believers turning the world upside down for Jesus. Let's face it: we should have more to be encouraged by than we do at present. Why do you suppose that is? Why do people who seem to start out following hard after God slip back into an unhealthy condition? Not to make excuses for those who weren't sincere, but I think there is a reason why some who have had a genuine encounter with Jesus have lost their enthusiasm.

I don't claim to know the whole explanation. But I think part of the answer is that many of today's sincere believers have lost their way in a theological maze. Many have invested themselves in causes that did not work out very well. The causes did not work because the focus was not on God's unchanging objective in every generation through history: building a family.

Do you know what happens when a sincere believer sets himself to run hard after God and serve Him with all his might, but finds that the path he's been running on has led to a dead end? He's not nearly as motivated when he changes direction and tries another path. Next time, he will only run at about three-fourths speed because he has a suspicion that this way might be futile as well. By the time he runs into three or four dead ends, he may decide to forget the whole thing and just sit down and lament his aching feet.

In order to run a good race and reach our destination, we must know what it is God wants to do with us. It's great to be able to run fast, but it's even more important to run smart. We have to know where we're going and how to get there. Only then will we be motivated not only to run hard but also to *keep* running.

As I started catching on to the importance of relationships, the various causes that had occupied my early Christian years began to be overshadowed. None of them seemed quite as important as before, though I kept hearing various leaders cling to their teachings and continue to promote them.

For me, they sort of slipped into the background. Replacing these causes was a sharper picture, one with brighter colors, richer texture. To be perfectly honest, watching this new picture take shape was a lot more satisfying. My increasingly deep conviction was that I was tapping into a truth I had not fully appreciated before. I began to devote myself more and more to the cause of helping build God's family.

CHAPTER 5

FOUNDATION
FOR RELATIONSHIP

Greater love has no one than this, that one lay down his life for his friends . . . I have called you friends.
—John 15:13,15

When you look more closely at the portrait of God's family, you will see the character of these people reflected in their faces. This family is satisfied with a fulfilling lifestyle, and their expressions reflect a joy that comes from walking closely with God and relating well with one another.

But has this family always been this close? Have they always been this happy? What have they had to go through, what have they had to learn to reach this point of satisfaction?

The truth is, once you get behind the scenes in the picture, you'll find that this family has had to travel a difficult, sometimes painful road. Their first step was to identify their "calling" as Christians.

A Christian's calling

Many believers struggle needlessly to discern a special "calling" on their lives or find a particular niche in the body of Christ. It can be a great relief to find that our highest calling is simply to pursue what is in God's heart: family. We all receive that calling; it's simply the call to be a Christian. It's the call to be rightly related to God and to one another.

We're now going to turn our attention to some principles in Scripture which form the foundation for relationships. Without this foundation, the picture on the puzzle box cannot be realized.

The book of Ephesians helps explain how central relationships are to our "calling." The first three chapters are filled with profound and comforting statements regarding our relationship with God. These passages speak of His great love for us, His eternal church, and the redeeming power exerted in our behalf through Jesus Christ. The last three chapters speak of the desire God has for us to have right relationships with our fellow believers. This section begins with an exhortation:

> I urge you to live a life worthy of the calling you have received.[1]

What follows are the Bible's instructions on how to do just that: live a life worthy of our calling. What does it talk about? Relationships. Be humble, it says. Be patient. Bear with one another in love. Speak truthfully to your neighbor. Do not sin when you are angry. Work, that you might share with those in need. Get rid of bitterness, rage, slander, malice. Be kind, forgiving, free from sexual immorality and greed. Husbands, love your wives; wives, respect your husbands. Children, obey your parents.

The passage sums up the instructions in this way:

> Be imitators of God, therefore, as dearly loved children and live a life of love, just as Christ loved us and gave himself up for us as a fragrant offering and sacrifice to God.[2]

A call to commitment

Our calling is not an opportunity to advance to the head table, flanking Jesus on His left or right, but to do what Jesus did: lay down our lives. We are called to a lifestyle of commitment. Sacrifice. Longsuffering. Loyalty. Through our life together, our life as a church, we're to manifest the kind of relationship God has with His church. This is the highest calling anyone can receive: to walk together in love with his brothers and sisters. Friendship is not merely the means of accomplishing the will of God; friendship *is* the will of God.

How do you know if you're living in a manner worthy of this calling? Ask yourself: Am I committed to a group of believers? Do I forgive? Am I patient and tenderhearted? Do I give to others a portion of what I have? Is my life, on my own and with my church, conducted in such a way that the unbelievers around me can understand the calling of a Christian? If you do not practice these things, then no matter how much you've prayed, no matter how much "ministry" you've accomplished, no matter how spiritually gifted you might be, you have fallen short of your calling as a Christian.

The local church context

The instructions on how to live a life worthy of our calling were not directed to specific individuals. All the New Testament epistles were written to the groups of believers who had come together in local churches. God chose this way of delivering His instructions because the church is His chosen instrument for expressing His life and message to the world.

Billy Graham, one of the greatest evangelists of this century, underscored the importance of the local church in his best-seller, *Approaching Hoofbeats.*

He [the apostle John, in Revelation] wrote to individual churches, small clusters of believers, leaders and followers together. At the heart of these letters is God's assumption that we belong together at work and at worship in a local church. I am convinced that the cluster of believers of which you are a part, those brothers and sisters in Christ with whom you join to pray and study, give and witness, is the basic unit through which God is working to redeem the world.[3]

God calls believers to come together in the church in such a way that their life together demonstrates the reality of Jesus.

Endurance or escape?

Relationships add pressure to our lives, and that pressure becomes intense at times. God uses relationships to test us: our patience, our humility, our longsuffering. And He tests whether we will be faithful to the calling of Christian life.

Have you ever been disgusted with someone in your church? Frustrated? Exasperated? Believe me, I have. I've awakened some mornings with my mind swirling with people's problems and problem people. I've stumbled out of bed, stared at my bloodshot eyes in the mirror, and started in on a gripe session. "Lord, I don't need this! You don't deserve these people. And neither do I!" (Do these sound like the words of one who understands his high calling as a servant of God?) At times like that, I can sympathize with the pastor who complained, "Lord, You've called me to pastor this church, but these people are hindering my calling!" But what is a pastor's calling? Is it to preach? To counsel? To marry and bury people? A pastor's first calling is the same as every Christian's: the call to love. This is a call to stick it out through thick and thin, for better or for worse. It's a call to persist even when you don't feel like it. It's a challenge to commit yourself to the people in your church.

If you don't accept that challenge, what happens when relationships get tough? When people make you mad? When people don't live up to your expectations? Will you be "called" somewhere else? God's calling isn't a quasi-religious excuse to escape tough times; it's a mandate to become as faithful a friend to others as God is to you.

God's calling does not separate us from people; it joins us together. The Bible compares the church to the parts of a human body: just as the heart is linked to the lungs and the arm to the hand, so are we linked to one another.[4] The local church was designed as a showcase in which to display the life of Jesus in a tangible way. The reality of Jesus is manifested when qualities such as kindness, forgiveness, and faithfulness are evident among us, holding the parts of the body together. In a love-starved world, the most convincing evidence that the gospel works is Christians who love one another.

The hostility disease

Unfortunately, we are seriously short of evidence. The reason is that we have contracted a deadly disease, the same ailment that plagued Cain. Cain farmed the soil, while his brother, Abel, tended the flocks; he brought the Lord his harvest as an offering, while his brother sacrificed the firstborn of his herds. The Lord looked favorably on Abel's offering, but not so with Cain's, and Cain became furious with his brother. Perhaps it was jealousy or envy that ignited his hatred. Whatever the cause, deep resentment rose within Cain, and he attacked his brother and killed him.

For the first family in history, it was not exactly an auspicious beginning. Yet this story is repeated again and again in the Bible—and it's repeated many times in the life of everyone—because the story of Cain is a story of the hostility that lies within us all. Human beings are, due to their fallen nature, prone to hostility. It takes many forms: anger, irritation, envy, jealousy, unforgiveness, bitterness. We use people. Betray people. We

seek to be first, even if we have to hurt others to do it. A poison
has seeped into our system, making us hostile toward God and
toward each other. The destructive potential of Cain lies within
all of us: history proves it; wars prove it; the need for law upon
law and still more law proves it. We prove it to ourselves, and
the church proves it to the world.

We can't turn over a new leaf and make our hostility go away;
we can't eliminate it with reason or willpower. Only God can put
our hostility to death. And that's what Jesus did on the cross: His
crucifixion crushed our enemy with a great death blow.[5]

So how do we take advantage of what Jesus has done? How
can the power of the cross deliver us from our hostility? Jesus laid
out the course plainly. "Follow Me," He said. Where does He tell
us to follow Him? To the cross. Jesus bids us to journey to Calvary
with Him because that is where we receive power to crush the
enemy within us. There, in our hearts, we stand before Christ
and see Him stretched out in agony for our sake. Then He
beckons us to become like Him in His death, that we might deal
our hostility a fatal blow and share in His life.

> If we have been united with him in his death, we will
> certainly also be united with him in his resurrection.
> For we know that our old self was crucified with him
> so that the body of sin might be rendered powerless.[6]

Crucifixion is the only cure for the disease that has afflicted
our family since the days of Cain. But this cure requires two
deaths: Jesus' and ours. The Bible speaks of two crosses, not one.
Jesus carried His cross, and He asks us to carry our cross. He was
emphatic about this. His instructions appear many times in
Scripture—twice just in the book of Luke:

> Then he said to them all: "If anyone would come after
> me, he must deny himself and take up his cross daily
> and follow me."[7]

And anyone who does not carry his cross and follow me cannot be my disciple.[8]

Crucifixion is the process of *making choices* that destroy selfishness and pride, allowing those traits to be replaced with love and humility.

Salvation is not God's ultimate goal for us. It is not the finish line; it is the starting line. A person can be saved and yet refuse to be transformed. His hostility will remain intact. At the altar of repentance we are forgiven, but not fully metamorphosed. Only crucifixion changes behavior.

The sparks fly

Jackie and Susan have dealt with hostility in their relationship. Jackie lived for a time with Susan, her husband, Joe, and their two small children. Susan worked full-time, and Jackie watched the children in exchange for room and board. To earn extra money, Jackie also babysat several other toddlers at their home.

Their relationship began one evening at McDonald's, when someone introduced them, and they struck up a conversation. As Susan explains, their personalities seemed to clash from the start.

> We came back from McDonald's, and I said to my husband, "I've found another person who's going to be important in my life."
>
> "How do you know?" he asked.
>
> "Because she drives me crazy," I said.
>
> The reason I would say that is that I don't think God gives us the privilege of not liking someone. You don't like someone? So what? Big deal. In the kingdom, what I like and what I don't like don't matter that much. Ultimately, we're obligated to a lot more than just "liking" people.

That evening Susan mentioned that she was returning to work after a leave of absence and was looking for a live-in babysitter. It turned out that Jackie was available. The pair spent several evenings talking about the situation and getting to know one another, and within a few weeks Jackie moved in. Before long tension began to build between them, as Susan explains.

> As it turned out, Jackie didn't like me that much, either. But we were in that relationship together, and we had to get through it.
>
> Jackie loves to cook, so she said, "Let me do the cooking." I said, "Certainly!" We thought everything was going to work out just fine. Jackie was in the house by herself every day with at least four kids under age four. After awhile, little things started happening that irritated me. We were living in a brand new house, and I would come home from work and find that it wasn't spic and span the way I'd left it. The walls were getting dirty. And I saw things that I thought shouldn't be happening.
>
> I thought she wasn't appropriately grateful for us letting her babysit other kids, who were tearing our house up. On the other hand, I wasn't at all grateful for what she was doing. I was just getting frustrated at what she wasn't doing. I thought to myself, "What's she got to do all day?" I had never been at home with kids, and I had no idea of what it takes. I guess I thought she was being lazy or irresponsible.
>
> Jackie would make dinner and want to leave, and that irritated me, too. Of course, now I know that if I've been in a house with six kids all day, I want to get out, too. When I first started staying home with my kids, it took about a month before I went to Jackie in tears and

said, "Forgive me, Jackie, I just didn't know. I only have two to deal with. You must have been working yourself to death!"

Jackie came over the other day and said, "Susan, I need somebody to be 'the heavy.' I need somebody to tell me the way it is." What she was saying is, "I'm going to expose a weakness to you, and I'm going to trust you with it."

There was a time in our relationship when we just showed what we thought was our best side because neither of us trusted the other with our weakness. Now I would trust her with anything.

Not only did God teach us what we needed to know, but he knit our hearts together. He caused us to love one another.

These two encountered the type of relationship obstacles all of us face. This type of story can easily end on a sour note; these two people, though, took the only available route—crucifixion—to get beyond hostility into friendship. Christianity that does not deal with this kind of relationship issue is not the Christianity of the Bible. The book of Ephesians says God is in the process of joining us, fitting people together like boards and nails, brick and mortar, to become a house in which He dwells. This is the message of the Bible. If the people in a church never form more than surface-deep relationships, if they never really get to know one another, then I don't think they should call themselves a church. They're not expressing the heart of God to a hurting world.

Spiritual lunacy

Now, of course, you can find Christians who say, "I don't need people. I just depend on the Spirit of God for my needs." That teaching has justified more lunacy in the church than we would like to admit. God puts His Spirit in people, so we can't cut ourselves off from God's people without cutting ourselves off from God.

If you need a piano moved, would you say something like this? "Oh, Jesus, please help me move my fifteen-hundred-pound piano. You know I depend upon You for my every need. I trust You in all situations and place no confidence in the arm of flesh."

Would the spirit of Samson suddenly come upon you, so that moving your concert grand would become a mere trifle?

More likely, as you wait for angels to be dispatched from heaven in response to your summons, you might get a phone call from someone in the church asking for your help with babysitting for the next Bible study meeting.

After agreeing to the babysitting, you tell the caller about how you are approaching your piano-moving task "in faith."

"I'm believing that God will give me the strength to move my piano," you say.

"Why haven't you called some men from the church to help?"

"Oh, I'm trusting God, not man. I've put my trust in man before and have only been disappointed."

The caller begins praying silently that you don't leave your babysitting responsibility to the angels, too.

Statements about looking to God, not man, to meet our needs may sound spiritual, but in truth they are a means of justifying our carnality so we can appear to be strong and self-sufficient. But the Spirit of God is not at work in us so that we can keep other people at arm's length and hide our weaknesses. He desires us to expose ourselves, share our needs that others might add to us the strength that God has supplied them.

God is not limited in how He works. In more than twenty years as a Christian, most of the comfort, strength, provision, instruction, and enjoyment I have received from God came through the frail channel of His people. These gifts are not lessened by passing through human hands, and the people who deliver them become precious to us. What a wise method of knitting us together.

Driven to the cross

The bottom line is that people need each other, and our need brings us together. And as people come together, their hostility is exposed—every time. It doesn't matter if it's a church or a Kiwanis Club, a Girl Scout troop, a high school football team, a Fortune 500 company, or a family. When people come together, everyone has to face the hostility within their hearts. God wants us to respond by running to the cross. And there, as we come face to face with what He has done for us, He asks us to do the same for others. To the degree that God has loved us, He asks us to love. To the degree that God has forgiven us, He asks us to forgive. To the degree that He has been patient with us, He asks us to be patient.

Embracing the second cross is not a one-time act, like throwing yourself on a grenade. We must make the hard choices day by day. God has made us in such a way that our need will drive us to Him again and again. When anger, resentment, or bitterness rises within us, we must die to it before the Lord.

It's easy to tell whether the people in a church have taken the message of the second cross to heart. If they have, their relationships will be sound and the church will work. If they haven't, then their hostility will be manifested over and over. People will gossip. They won't accept those different from themselves. They will complain and bicker and be easily offended. They won't be able to work together or minister together. If this is the case, they have not allowed the cross to have an effect on their lives, and their testimony to the world is greatly diminished.

Jesus prayed, "May they be brought to complete unity to let the world know that you sent me."[9] The world will know we are

Christians by our unity, by our love for one another, by the absence of hostility among us. Only the church can show a hostile world that God has a remedy for its fear and pain. That is why relationships among believers are so significant.

Alarm bells should ring if you are still easily offended, if you cannot accept correction, if you just can't seem to get along with people. If this describes your relationships, you haven't embraced the second cross, and you will not be effective in the church.

On becoming a faithful friend

Jesus' disciples were an unlikely mix. He sought out fishermen, a rough and rugged breed of men; tax collectors—the "white collar" accountant-types of His day; and a variety of others, bringing them together to share His life, not just His thoughts. They ate, slept, worked, prayed, laughed, and cried together. In the process, Jesus made them His friends. Jesus was the Master Friend. Through His relationships with these men, He showed us what constitutes friendship of the highest level. No greater love is possible, Jesus said, than the love shown to a friend:

> My command is this: Love each other as I have loved you. Greater love has no one than this, that one lay down his life for his friends.[10]

Obviously, if the theme of the Bible is relationship, then we ought to perk up when we read Jesus talking about His own friendships and what it means to be a friend. In John's gospel, Jesus explains how His disciples became His friends.

> I no longer call you servants, because a servant does not know his master's business. Instead, I have called you friends, for everything that I learned from my Father I have made known to you.[11]

The role of a servant (some translations use the word *slave*) is simply to follow orders, to get the job done, no questions asked. The master never reveals his reasoning or shares why he makes certain demands. He rarely exposes his thoughts or feelings. He remains aloof, separate, safe.

Our relationships often can be like that: we want to protect ourselves at all costs from being exposed; we venture nothing that might make us feel vulnerable; we keep our distance. But Jesus did not relate to His disciples that way. Rather, He exposed His inner life to His disciples. After Jesus ministered to the multitudes, He withdrew with His band of friends, answered their questions, and explained everything plainly. He revealed who He was and why He did what He did. He held nothing back. And as Jesus revealed Himself, He made these men His friends.

The hiding place

When we share our inner lives with others we establish that link of relationship. It is risky business to make that connection because it makes us vulnerable. When we expose our inner selves, we are taking a chance with people. We're counting on them not to take advantage of us, not to turn on us or use what we have said against us. We are taking a gamble that they will be true friends: loyal, dependable, trustworthy. Many of us look at the odds, and say, "Forget it. It's too big a risk." But Jesus did not.

The faithfulness choice

For Jesus, the faithfulness of others was not an issue in whether or not to establish a friendship. He chose to be a faithful friend, and that choice did not depend on His friends holding up their end. In fact, they did not: they failed Him miserably.

In the Garden of Gethsemane, Jesus faced His most desperate hour. He asked His friends to stay close and pray with Him. They slept. He awakened them three times and asked them again to pray with Him; each time they went back to sleep. When the soldiers came to take Him to His execution, all His friends left Him. How painful that must have been for Him.

If we take the risk Jesus took, we can expect to bear some of the pain He bore. If we venture out in friendship, we can expect that some people will wound us. People will let us down. They will disappoint us. We will feel heartache. That's all part of the cost of friendship.

The price of friendship

To create the kind of family God desires, people have to work at getting along. They have to learn to deal with their hostility: overlooking faults, forgiving hurts, laying down expectations. They have to learn to look for what they can give in friendships rather than what they can receive. They have to be committed to resolving resentments and relational impasses.

Phil and Brad, both leaders in our church, can testify that relationships get tough sometimes. They have passed over some difficult ground in their fourteen-plus years together. Phil explains:

> I tell people that Brad and I have been to hell and back. But I figure that if I can go to hell and back with a guy, I can go anywhere, can't I? The Lord went to hell and back for us, and who's going to separate us from His love?
>
> I don't think there is anything we can't work out. We've gone through living together; problems between our wives and how that affects each of us; problems between ourselves and our ministries; how we perceive each other; how we see how others perceive us. We went through a period when we didn't really

communicate for two years. We weren't sure that we ever wanted to. If we ever reconciled, who was to say that we wouldn't have to live with that pain? But we decided that we were going to live together for the rest of our lives—and for the rest of eternity—so we had better work things out.

No doubt about it, relationships are challenging. Sometimes God puts us with people whose ways of doing things are altogether different from our own. Maybe we find certain people hard to work with. Maybe they're too outspoken or too polite. Maybe they're too precise or not precise enough, too formal or too casual. Our differences, though, really do not matter. We have to get to the point where we can say, "You are my brothers and sisters. I'm committed to you. I'm committed to expressing the heart of God. I'm ready to lose my life for Jesus' sake and for the sake of those with whom God has put me. This is my priority: the family that God is creating."

We cannot, however, force relationships any more than we can make ourselves happy. It's a curious paradox: if we seek friendship for friendship's sake, we often come away empty-handed. Like happiness, the more you seek relationships, the more elusive they become. Happiness is the result and benefit of serving God. Likewise, meaningful relationships come not by seeking them directly, but by seeking a higher calling: meeting the needs of others.

A 'people' person

Perhaps you are a person who says, "I just can't relate to people." Or, "I'm not a 'people' person." Or "I'm most comfortable when I'm by myself." Well, Jesus was not asking us to do something that comes naturally to us. We need to recognize our need for change, and then cry out to God to change us that we might become faithful friends. God might ask you to die to lifelong habits, patterns, or preferences that hinder you from pursuing relationships with the people in your church. It might take a dramatic change in your thinking.

You may have to sacrifice a great deal for the sake of this relationship kingdom. Laying down your life for your friends is a matter of investing yourself in people's lives. That will tax your emotions; it will drain your energy; it will deplete your free time. It will require you to do things that you don't feel like doing; it will not be pleasing to your flesh. But that is the cost of laying a foundation that can make right relationships become a reality.

So although the picture we've discussed looks like one big happy family, each person has paid a price to be included in the portrait.

CHAPTER 6

REALITY
OF RELATIONSHIPS

In the early years of our fellowship, as the picture of a family was coming into sharper focus, we concentrated almost exclusively on relationships. The cornerstone of our church was—and is—the conviction that when you boil down the message of the Bible, everything has to do with relationships, based on love, with God and with others. We talked about servanthood, about laying down our lives for each other, about seeking our brother's highest good. As time went by we sensed more and more cohesion as a church.

Shortly after we moved into our first building, the mother of one of the young women in our congregation paid me one of the highest compliments I've ever received. She made a comment confirming that some of our teaching had taken hold. When her daughter was planning her wedding at our church, the mother had expressed some concern about having it in our building.

"It's not a *real* church," the mother complained.

I knew what she meant. Our building did not look much like a traditional church. In fact, with neither steeple nor stained glass, people have joked that the outside looks like a racquetball club.

After the wedding the bride's mother came up to me and expressed her amazement at how kind everyone had been. Dozens of people had volunteered to help with the food, clean-up, and other arrangements. Her attitude had made a 180-degree turn.

"You really have something here," she said.

"Well, we have a family," I replied.

"That's it!" she said. "It's just like a family."

The vision taking shape in our hearts was of the spiritual family God wanted us to be, and we did not want to have just a collection of independently operating Christians who happened to go to the same church. We wanted to be a community of believers "rightly" related to God and to each other. Our desire was to be genuinely bonded together, not just by a common creed or doctrine or by participating in the same religious activities, but by a dependence on God and each other.

Knowing God

Knowing God has been a major theme of ours. No amount of "religious" activity can replace a personal relationship with God. Our God is a Father who desires to have fellowship with His children. He wants us to be intimate with Him, sharing our innermost thoughts and feelings with Him. God promises to draw close to us as we draw close to Him. He wants to reveal Himself to us, that we might share His burdens, His emotions, His desires.

We have found that these two "pillars" of relationship—loving God and loving one another—cannot be separated. We can't love God without loving our brothers and sisters; and we can't love each other without loving God and accepting His help. Our sinfulness, the basic self-centeredness of human nature, renders us incapable of the kind of relationships God desires, even when we form relationships with people to whom we are naturally attracted. God has placed this natural yearning for relationships within us, but by ourselves we lack the ability it takes to make relationships last over the long haul. So in striving for lasting, consistently loving relationships we are drawn into a deeper relationship with God, because only He can supply the necessary building materials.

Volumes have been written about the principles of godly

relationships, but I would like to describe how these principles have become a reality in the lives of people in our church. Clay, now on our pastoral team, has been part of the church for more than a decade. He talks from his own experience about knowing the Lord.

Our relationship with God begins as a huge mystery because we're dealing with a personality that's not like any we've ever known. The relationship is in some ways like the one we have with our parents, and spouses, and others who love us, but in other ways it's also very unlike those relationships. It's not long before we realize that if we are to know God, He must reveal Himself to us.

Strange as it might sound, I've also found that we have to show God who we are, too. As we get to know Him, we come to know ourselves in a deeper way. As we're going through life, we recognize things in ourselves that we don't want God to know about. We just don't want to be that real with Him, and that brings the relationship to a standstill.

This kind of standstill can happen in a marriage, too, when one partner feels that the other will never know him or her beyond a certain level. The only way to get through that is to reveal more about yourself—to take a bigger risk, to attempt to be more intimate—even though everything in you tells you it's useless because that person won't understand.

I've had problems that I haven't wanted to talk over with my wife. Either I didn't think it would do any good or I was too embarrassed to admit I even had the problem. But no matter how much I prayed about it, it wouldn't go away. The only way I got over that hurdle was to expose the problem. Only then would it get better.

Our relationship with the Lord is like that. We reach

plateaus, and if we just leave the relationship there it begins to die. To move forward we have to talk to the Lord about topics that are more embarrassing, more difficult, less enjoyable to deal with. But the more real we become with Him, the more real He becomes with us.

Reading the Bible is also paramount in getting to know God. It's using an outside resource, an objective standard, to fill our hearts with the thoughts of God. When you try to live out the Word of God, then immediately you run into problems. It's like what happens when my wife sends me to the store; I think I understand what she wants until I get into the aisle and see all the choices. We think we understand God's Word until we begin to live it; then we end up with a lot of questions.

For example, if we're talking about forgiveness, we say, "Lord, what do you mean by forgive? Do you mean I have to forgive even *this?* Do you mean forgive so that I don't have any hard feelings toward this person anymore? Do you mean forgive and forget?" All the questions that come as we try to do God's will lead us into a deeper understanding of God's heart.

As we stay in contact with people who love God, He relates also with us through them, sometimes even unbeknown to them. He causes them to say and do certain things. While the act comes through them, it is clearly God responding through them to something we've been talking to Him about. To sum it up, then, I've found that my relationship with God deepens through confession and prayer, through the reading of the Word, through fellowship and through trying to do His will.

Living together

In the midst of the ongoing emphasis on intimate relationships with God, we began exploring different ways of cultivating relationships among ourselves as well. Some years back, Clay was the leader of a "brothers' house" for single men in our church. Rather than pursue independent lifestyles, young men moved into a large house where they prayed regularly together, ate meals together, and generally shared their lives. The church also had "sisters' houses," and like the brothers' houses, the focus was on growing in the Lord and developing healthy relationships.

One member of Clay's house was John. He moved to Columbia in 1979, when he was twenty-five, to attend law school. He wanted to live in one of the brothers' houses, but he had reservations about living in a house that required a high level of commitment: he would be putting twenty to thirty hours a week into house-related activities. John was hesitant, but with few other housing options he decided to give it a try.

The house was just getting started, and many details needed to be ironed out. The seven housemates spent a long time sorting out the issues. When Clay, the man in charge, made a suggestion, John usually responded with an idea of his own he liked better. But that began to change.

> In the beginning, whenever I disagreed with something that was happening I would speak up. Rather than doing what I was asked, I just became one more voice of strife.
>
> After awhile, I saw that our little discussions weren't working; we just needed to hear one voice and follow it. So I began to hold my tongue and support Clay, and did my best to die to all the emotions that were pulling me in other directions.
>
> I was restless during that period of my life. I wasn't interested in sticking with anything too long, and God began to deal with me about commitment. Because that first semester in the house was especially difficult, I wanted to move out. I'd tell the Lord, "This isn't

working. It's time to leave, isn't it, Lord?" I'd hear dead silence from heaven. The awful feeling would come over me that I was supposed to stay—and do some more dying.

One of John's lessons would be learned from a roommate with different housecleaning habits from his:

> I had a sloppy roommate who would leave clothes all over. Sometimes I could hardly walk in our room. It seemed a lot less trouble to move out than to get this guy to change. But I felt God challenging me to stay with this brother, even if his clothes were piled so high I had to tunnel my way to bed.
>
> God was telling me that neatness wasn't the most important thing in my roommate's life at that moment. I needed to accept his sloppiness and try to encourage him in the areas where God was dealing with him.
>
> God was calling me to commit myself to my brothers to a greater degree. I felt Him asking me, "Will you stay here as long as I want you to, without putting any deadline on it?" I could see myself still there at age sixty, waiting for God to let me go. But I promised God I would stay until He released me. I ended up staying four years.

John stuck it out with this group of people who had different backgrounds and little in common other than a desire to serve God. Ultimately, the perseverance paid off:

> We didn't want to spend much time with each other because the relationships were tough. But we kept on trying because we knew God wanted us to, and eventually we found that we became one. We became a group of people who, in general, loved being with each other.

Throughout the church, people have a desire to go beyond the superficial relationships of the world. For the sake of relationships, people are willing to go beyond what is comfortable and convenient, to the point of sharing their houses, their possessions, and their privacy with others. It has become commonplace for families to open their homes to others. A family might host a foreign couple visiting the church for the summer, or might use a spare bedroom or basement to house a Bible college student, a young person, or a single mother with a young child. Families often move in with another family for several weeks or months while they're waiting to build or buy a house. These various living arrangements have served as a boot camp for relationships and have helped knit our church together.

Phil, one of the church's pastoral leaders, recalls one of his living situations in which six adults and two children shared the same house. It was no bed of roses, as he explains:

> We got to know one another. It was hard. It was real hard. There is a lot of carnality in people. We had fights. We struggled through things. I could spit nails at people, I got so mad. Things got out of hand at times.
>
> We had to get along with everybody's idiosyncrasies, and that was hard. And we had to deal with our attitudes. You can't hide your attitudes when you live with people. They become pretty obvious.
>
> As we approached the end of the first year, we all couldn't wait to get out. You could just tell that feeling was there: "Boy, I'm glad this year is over." Then when the time came, we all decided that we hadn't allowed God to deal with us like we should have, that we needed to live together longer.

The practical art of family living

The group of young people that once fit in our living room had grown into a church of 150 or more adults in a few years. No matter how large we grew, we did not want to lose our family-style fellowship. To be sure everyone had the opportunity to get beyond the Sunday-morning acquaintance level, we divided the church into "small groups." These groups meet every week or two in members' homes and provide a casual way for people to get to know each other.

Finding themselves side by side are teenagers and retired couples, auto mechanics and university professors, trailer park residents and people who live in $100,000 houses. Get-togethers usually involve worship, Bible study or teaching, prayer, and a time of sharing. Activities vary widely, but the main emphasis is on relationships: getting to know and enjoy one another, letting down barriers, sharing joys and hurts, exposing personal and spiritual needs, praying for the needs of others, and providing practical support.

Michelle, a single mother, was in a small group when she encountered a personal crisis. She had been in the church about a year and a half when she picked up a virus from her work at a local hospital. She had to spend a lot of time in bed, and during her several-week recovery time, she couldn't take care of her day-to-day responsibilities. A number of people came over during that period to help clean the house, prepare meals, mow the lawn, and care for her six-year-old daughter. "The experience was one of having a family," Michelle said.

The church was becoming a "family" to many. Beyond the practical help provided, people were experiencing, through their brothers and sisters in the church, God's kindness, forgiveness, and faithfulness.

Thom and Ronda became part of the church when they moved to Columbia, where Thom could pursue a master's degree in forestry at the University of Missouri. Their cross-country move from Idaho had eaten up all their savings, and they had nothing to fall back on. With a wife and three children, Thom had to make ends meet with the money he earned from his graduate-student assistantship. That paid the rent and bought the groceries, but left little else. They had no health insurance, and when Ronda became pregnant with their fourth child, it was a considerable financial hardship.

They went hospital shopping, trying to find the cheapest place to have a child. The state-owned hospital offered to discount its standard $2,000 charge to $1,000 because of their financial crunch. But the offer came with one stipulation: the money had to be paid before the delivery.

Thom and Ronda had been attending a small group for a month or two when this crisis hit. They hardly knew anyone because they were so new, but small-group members chipped in $800 to help pay off their hospital bill.

To further complicate matters, Ronda became ill; for about three months she could not take care of the kids or her household tasks. The family lived ten miles north of town, but a continual flow of people went to help out during their crisis. Ronda talks about the impact of this support:

> People would just come. People we didn't know would come to help us. People who had no reason other than the love of Christ to reach out to us would come and do things for us and take care of the kids.
>
> I didn't have any maternity clothes, and people provided them. They pretty well took care of us. And people didn't just do things, but they were kind and loving. They gave their hearts as well. It was really hard for me to accept it all because I wasn't used to people treating me like that, and I wasn't able to respond to it. I would just watch.
>
> I would write my friend back home in Idaho and tell her about what it was like to be in this church that had a vision. I had never been in a church where there was a vision, a driving force, a motivation behind what the people were doing. They weren't just saying, "Well, let's do a good deed." There was a purpose behind what they were doing, a godly purpose that really drew our hearts. We saw a vision of the church working as

it's really supposed to work. We saw that it was real.
They lived it out for us.

This couple, along with the other people you've heard from
in this chapter, were hearing in the services a constant stream of
teaching about relationships. But the goal of instruction is not
simply to educate the hearers about truth. The goal, as the
apostle Paul wrote, is to stimulate the hearers to live a practical
life of love "from a pure heart, a good conscience, and a sincere
faith."[1]

We hear many churches described as "Bible-believing" and
"Christ-centered." But beyond the theological labels, how can
we tell if a congregation is living up to these claims? By reading
the church's articles of faith? By listening to the Sunday morning
sermon?

Very simply, I believe you will find all the evidence you need
by examining the quality of their relationships.

CHAPTER
7

THE PUZZLE
PRINCIPLES

For several years of my Christian walk, two-thirds of the Bible seemed clouded with confusion. Only the last third, the New Testament, was somewhat comprehensible. It was in the New Testament that I found the most straightforward scriptures about loving God and each other, about the centrality of relationships in the Christian life.

Admittedly, I did not have a clue to what the Old Testament was all about. I felt lost reading the Pentateuch, the first five books of the Bible. I could barely even get through Leviticus, with its laborious rules and regulations for Jewish society. The major prophets, like Isaiah and Jeremiah, and the minor prophets, like Joel and Malachi, spoke in shrouded mysteries. I generally had no idea what they were talking about. In fact, in those days we saw so little relevance in the Old Testament that the Bibles we carried only included the New Testament, perhaps with Psalms and Proverbs.

The Israel emphasis

While many preachers claimed to understand the maze of Old Testament history and prophecy and how it applied to twentieth-century affairs, their interpretations made little sense to me. I did notice one thing about the Old Testament, though: all the books seemed to be centered around one nation—Israel. The Law was given to Israel. The prophets rebuked Israel for its backsliding but also spoke awesome promises to that nation. Israel, for some reason, was singled out from all the nations of the earth as the focal point of God's involvement in human affairs.

Some Christians were taught to revere the Jewish nation to the point that these people seemed far more significant in the biblical scheme of things than believers grouped in churches throughout the earth. Not only were the Jews the focal point of biblical history, they apparently were to be at the center of the end-times events as well. This mentality has had a deep effect on the present-day church.

I had no problem believing that Israel was important, but that left me with more questions. Where do Christians fit in? What role does the church have to play in the overall scheme of things?

The Bible emphatically states that Israel is God's most treasured possession. Since it was considered that a nation on the other side of the world was of primary importance to God, did that mean that Christians were of only secondary importance? I had already learned that God above all else wants a family of people who love Him and each other. These two ideas—God's love for Israel and His desire for a family—had seemed completely disjointed, but now I was beginning to see a most significant connection. It was a startling thought, but I began considering the possibility that these two expressions of God's purpose were not so different after all.

It was against the backdrop of God's passionate devotion to the Jewish people and the nation of Israel that I came across some troubling passages in the New Testament. As we begin looking at some of these passages, let me offer a brief warning that some challenging theological terrain lies ahead. I am aware that some of the statements you will read here may contrast with some deeply cherished views. But all I can tell you is that when I stripped off the veneer of a relatively modern system of theological interpretation and tried to look at the raw truth of the Bible, I saw a different picture from the one generally promoted today. This new picture is one in which the true Israel of God's choosing is a spiritual family, the church.[1]

Some have said that in my discussions about the role of Israel in God's plan, I have created a tempest in a teapot. "What's the big deal?" they wonder. I suppose that at first it may not seem that significant. But considering the emphasis the Bible places on Israel, I think it is fair to assume that recognizing the identity of this nation will help us understand what God is doing with us today and throughout history. The implications of this issue, as you will see, are enormous. For some of you this material may help sort out issues that have been confusing for years, and you may arrive at some stirring, life-changing conclusions.

Some troubling issues

Since I was surrounded by the teaching that places the geographical nation of Israel at the heart of God's purpose, the following issues created some serious questions for me:

1. When John the Baptist was addressing the natural Jews of his day—the leaders, in fact—he didn't seem to consider their position very secure. When the Jewish leaders claimed special standing with God because they were children of Abraham, John replied that their natural heritage was worthless. God could raise up children for Abraham from stones, he told them.[2]

2. Later, Jesus went a step further. He had a similar encounter in which the Jewish leaders claimed that their father was Abraham, therefore providing for them a special relationship with God. But Jesus denied that they were related to Abraham. He said they had a different father: the devil.[3] Jesus was not saying that these Jews couldn't trace their *natural* lineage to Abraham; He was saying they couldn't trace their *spiritual* lineage to Abraham. Evidently He was saying that these men were not part of Abraham's nation because they were not, like Abraham, men of faith.

3. The apostle Paul raised a provocative point when, in Romans 2:28, he said that "he is not a Jew who is one outwardly, but he is a Jew who is one inwardly. . . . Circumcision is of the heart."
4. Galatians 3 indicates that Jews, like everyone else, have always had but one means of coming to God: by faith.

> Consider Abraham: "He believed God, and it was credited to him as righteousness." Understand, then, that those who believe are children of Abraham. . . . Clearly no one is justified before God by the law, because, "The righteous will live by faith." [4]

This statement identifies Abraham's children as those who have lived by faith in God—not those who have relied on the law and their natural heritage for their salvation.

5. Galatians 4 divides the Jewish people into two groups. The descendants of Hagar, the slave who gave birth to Ishmael through natural conception, are said to represent the Jews who lived by the law rather than by faith. They are considered slaves. The descendants of Isaac, the son born supernaturally through God's promise, are said to represent the people of faith. This passage says that the slaves—those without faith—are excluded from the inheritance because they are not sons at all; the people of faith are the sole heirs.

What does the Scripture say?

> Get rid of the slave woman and her son, for the slave woman's son will never share in the inheritance with the free woman's son. [5]

To sort out the questions raised by these passages and many others like them, I had to have some principles to give me direction in the search for answers. I have ended up with three primary principles that have helped clarify the picture on the box of the puzzle, that picture God wants to use to guide us in our lives.

Puzzle Principle No. 1:
The New Interprets the Old

When I ran across these New Testament scriptures speaking about Israel and the Jews, I realized that I could not turn my back on the Old Testament. Jesus, John the Baptist, and the apostles seemed to challenge the conventional thinking of their day about Israel, bringing a radically different perspective. I wanted to be sure I understood what they were saying, and to do so I needed to be familiar with the Old Testament.

The first question that needs to be addressed is this: What is the relationship between the Old and New Testaments? Like many, at first I assumed that the New Testament in a sense replaced the Old. Many thought the Old Covenant had passed away and had been replaced by the New Covenant, rendering the Law and the Prophets virtually obsolete. Many figured that most of Old Testament teaching didn't apply to people born after Jesus. It made for a good history lesson, but since everything changed so much when Jesus came, some thought they would be on safer ground if they stuck mainly with the New Testament.

In studying Scripture, though, I began to notice that the New Testament writers didn't see it that way. Instead, they quoted the Old Testament extensively, often pulling out passages and explaining what those passages meant. Though at times it seems like the two sections of the Bible are incompatible, I concluded that these two "testaments" are not separate, unconnected bodies of information. They have equal standing as the authoritative Word of God. So how do we make sense of Moses, Isaiah, and Malachi? *By looking back into the Old Testament through the eyes of Jesus and the writers of the New Testament.*[6]

I have heard a rhyme on this theme that makes a lot of sense:

> The New is in the Old contained;
> the Old is in the New explained.
> The New is in the Old concealed;
> the Old is in the New revealed.

How can we be so confident that the New Testament interprets the Old? How can we be sure that God gave the proper interpretation of the Old Testament to the writers of the New? To put it briefly, we can be sure because that is what the Bible itself says.

The road to Emmaus

Late in the afternoon of the day Jesus rose from the dead, two of His disciples were walking to a small town called Emmaus. Distraught and confused over the uproar of the last few days, they were desperately trying to make sense of the recent events when a third man joined them on the road. The conversation among the three of them went something like this:

"What's been going on around here that has caused you to be so sad?" asks the man who joins the travelers.

"What's been going on?" they repeat incredulously. "Where have you been? You're the only one around here who doesn't know." They explain that Jesus, whom they believed was the Christ, was executed by the Romans. Now, though, some of their friends have been saying they have seen Him alive.

Weary and disheartened, the disciples go on. "To tell you the truth, we don't know what to think."

The man keeps baiting them with questions. Finally he grows impatient with their answers; it is clear they do not understand the Scriptures. "O foolish men and slow of heart to believe in all that the prophets have spoken. . . ." They walk together for the next couple of hours, and Jesus interprets the Bible for them.

> And beginning with Moses and all the Prophets, he explained to them what was said in all the Scriptures concerning himself.[7]

In *all* the Scriptures, the verse says. These disciples got the clear picture of what is on the front of that puzzle box, down to the most minute detail. How would you like to have a chance to walk seven miles with Jesus, listening to Him explain the entire Bible to you? That would beat reading this book, wouldn't it?

Later on, when these same disciples had returned to Jerusalem and were telling the others of their encounter with Jesus, the Lord visited them again. At this time He explained to the future apostles that what had happened to Him was in fulfillment of God's Word; and then, "he opened their minds so they could understand" the Old Testament.[8]

That is a powerful verse. It says that only God can open our minds to the Bible. Only God can show us the complete picture. The apostles—several of whom would be involved in writing books of the New Testament—were appointed by God and given revelation by Him with which they unveiled the mysteries of the Old Testament.

The apostle Paul said he was also given special "insight into the mystery of Christ, which was not made known to men in other generations as it has now been revealed to God's holy apostles and prophets."[9] These were the people who really "understood" the Scriptures. The religious leaders did not understand; they knew the Scriptures backward and forward, yet failed to comprehend the message.

Jesus gave the New Testament authors the accurate perspective on Israel, its history and the prophecies regarding its future. He revealed to them the proper interpretation of all that had been written. Peter, one of the New Testament writers, said that the Old Testament prophets had only partial understanding of their prophecies, but that the Spirit of Christ within them showed them glimpses of the future.[10] Clearly, we do not have the ability, or the liberty, to interpret the Old Testament ourselves. The point is, we must not allow anyone to give us an interpretation of the Old Testament that is contrary to the writings of the New Testament. The New Testament writers themselves are the only infallible interpreters.

Puzzle Principle No. 2:
The Mind Set on the Flesh Is Death

Let me start the discussion of this second principle with some questions. Why can't we understand the Old Testament unless God reveals it? Why couldn't the scribes and Pharisees understand the purpose of God? Why were the disciples blinded to the meaning of the Bible until Jesus explained it? Why was I so confused about the Old Testament, the role of Israel in God's plan? Why is there so much emotion over this issue? Why are there so many differing opinions over this issue?

I think those questions can all be answered by one simple statement found in the epistle written to the Romans by a man who met Jesus face to face. The apostle Paul, who encountered Jesus on the road to Damascus, sought to explain to the Roman church the role of Jew and Gentile in the plan of God. In this explanation he made a radical statement, which forms the second puzzle principle:

For the mind set on the flesh is death.[11]

Death, he said. He equated a mentality, a way of looking at something, with a state we all dread, a state that represents the end of life itself. This must be a pretty horrid way of thinking if he compared it to death. So perhaps we should make sure we understand what he means by "the mind set on the flesh."

Fortunately, he explains further. He says the mind set on the flesh is "hostile to God" and that those who are in the flesh "cannot please God." We are severely warned not to set our minds on the flesh, and are instructed in the same passage to set our minds on the Spirit. Only the Spirit-centered mind obtains life and peace.

Flesh and spirit

To help sort this out a little further, let's define flesh and spirit in this way:

1. *Flesh:* that which originates within man and is sustained by man.

2. *Spirit:* that which originates in God and is sustained by God.

In sum, that which God produces is spirit; that which man produces is flesh.

Let me ask a critical question. Do you think the Bible is a spiritual book or a natural book? When we read the Bible, should our minds be set on the flesh or on the spirit?

This is the question that Jesus asked Nicodemus when the Jewish teacher sought Him out one night. Nicodemus was an honorable man, highly respected among his countrymen. And he was not antagonistic toward Jesus; he even recognized that Jesus had come from God. But he had questions; he had some things he wanted to get settled. So he slipped away one night to seek out the Rabbi Jesus.

When Nicodemus found Him, he initiated one of the most important conversations recorded in the Bible. He asked, in effect, "Who are You, Jesus, and what are You teaching?"

Jesus recognized the sincerity of the question, but He knew it was futile to answer it. Why? Because Nicodemus saw through eyes of flesh, interpreting spiritual teaching in terms of natural things. So Jesus answered in a way that bewildered Nicodemus.

"Unless a man is born again, he cannot see the kingdom of God."[12] I can picture Nicodemus thinking, "How preposterous! Can a man get back into his mother's womb?" Of course he had completely missed the point.

Jesus gets to His point: "That which is born of flesh is flesh. That which is born of the spirit is spirit," saying that only those who go through the spiritual birth process, and who then view Scripture through spiritual eyes, can enter and understand the kingdom of God.

Jesus gave Nicodemus a lesson in Bible interpretation: viewing truth through the eyes of flesh is futile. It only leads to confusion.[13] The only way to understand the kingdom of God is by seeing its truths through the eyes of the spirit. Likewise, the Bible is a spiritual book. It can only be understood by those who look at it through spiritual eyes.

Puzzle Principle No. 3:
Shadows Lead to Substance

The third principle helping to bring the picture on the puzzle box into focus has to do with the relationship between a shadow and the object responsible for casting that shadow.

Imagine yourself standing still on a bright summer day in the late afternoon or early evening. If the sun is behind you, you will cast a long shadow straight ahead. Someone comes along, staring straight down at the ground, and notices the shadow. Intrigued, the person examines it, noticing what looks like the outline of a head, then shoulders. Following the shadow, he steps toward what appears to be a torso, then hips, then legs.

What has this person learned about you so far? Not very much. He does not know your name, how you think, why you are there or what you are planning to do.

The information contained in the Old Testament does not answer the questions; it just exposes the shadow. That shadow is cast by the person who is the main subject of the New Testament: Jesus. To read the Old Testament by itself and draw conclusions about spiritual truths is mere guesswork. You might hit on a few items, but chances are you would be wrong in your major conclusions, just like Nicodemus, just like the disciples on the road to Emmaus before Jesus explained things to them.

Paul taught the Colossians that the Old Testament rituals were a mere shadow pointing to Christ:

> Therefore do not let anyone judge you by what you eat or drink, or with regard to a religious festival, a New Moon celebration or a Sabbath day. These are a shadow of the things that were to come; the reality, however, is found in Christ.[14]

What were some of the parts—the "arms and legs," so to speak—of the shadow cast in the Old Testament? Let's consider an example.

At one point during the Hebrew nation's trek through the wilderness, the people were being bitten by serpents and were dying from the poison. God told Moses to take a pole, put a bronze serpent on top of it, and lift it up. When anyone bitten by a serpent looked to the pole, God told him, that person would be healed.

Now what in the world does that mean? Going back to the New Testament discourse between Jesus and Nicodemus, Jesus explained that He Himself was casting the shadow in the Old Testament:

> Just as Moses lifted up the snake in the desert, so the Son of Man must be lifted up, that everyone who believes in him may have eternal life.[15]

That verse comes immediately before one of the most quoted verses in the Bible, John 3:16.[16] So what is the significance of the incident with the bronze serpent? It is that the snake on the pole was a shadow of God's beloved Son on the cross, the only cure for the venom of sin. If we try to assign more meaning to the actual, natural occurrence in the Old Testament, we will be lost in the shadow, never arriving at the substance.

Now if you follow this principle through the Old Testament, you will find lots of shadows cast by Jesus: the water that came out of the rock, the blood on the door posts in Egypt, the lambs that were slain before the first Passover, Abraham preparing to sacrifice his only son, the prophets' and kings' zeal for the house of God. These events all point to Christ. And they all lose their meaning if you focus on the shadow and ignore the substance. Once the substance has arrived, we no longer need to speculate on the meaning of the shadows.

CHAPTER
8

THE FAMILY
OF GOD

Israel is a nation of about four million people situated on the eastern Mediterranean coast. Its name is mentioned on the evening news nearly every night. I think it's safe to say that no other nation in the modern world stirs up such strong sentiments of either passionate love or passionate hatred.

Israel is also mentioned in Scripture more than 2,500 times. Read the Bible, starting in Genesis, and very quickly you will reach the time in human history where Israel becomes the focal point of the events recorded. From the days of Abraham on, Israel is the nation God has "chosen" to demonstrate His way of life to the human community. God sets His nation apart as His treasured possession, and declares it the greatest of all nations.[1]

Not only was Israel's role critical in the historical events recorded in the Bible, but the prophets also spoke frequently about Israel's role in the future. Leaf through the Old Testament, and you will come across dozens of passages indicating Israel's continued prominence in history. Consider, for example, this passage in Deuteronomy:

> The Lord will open the heavens, the storehouse of His bounty, to send rain on your land in season and to bless all the work of your hands. You will lend to many

nations but will borrow from none. The Lord will make
you the head, not the tail. If you pay attention to the
commands of the Lord your God that I give you this day
and carefully follow them, you will always be at the
top, never at the bottom.[2]

Israel is unmistakably a key player in God's plan. But this
factor raises the question we addressed in the last chapter: What
is Israel? Is it a nation made up of citizens of the same religion
or the same ethnic stock? Is it the country in which that nation
lives? Or is it something else?

The Middle East passion

Many in recent decades have given much attention, prayer,
sympathy, and money to the Middle Eastern nation that was
reestablished in 1948. Popular interest in Israel was heightened
by Hal Lindsey's best-seller, *The Late Great Planet Earth*. One of
the book's main themes is that the re-establishment of Israel as
a nation is a historic signpost heralding the imminent return of
Christ:

> The one event which many Bible students in the past
> overlooked was this paramount prophetic sign: Israel
> had to be a nation again in the land of its forefathers.
> . . . A dream for so many years, [Israel was] made a
> reality on 14 May 1948 when David Ben-Gurion read
> the Declaration of Independence announcing the
> establishment of a Jewish nation to be known as the
> State of Israel.[3]

Many like Lindsey believed that 1988 was a benchmark in the
fulfillment of end-times prophecy, since it marked the fortieth
year from Israel's rebirth as a nation. One writer even went so
far as to predict that the Second Coming would coincide with the

year of Israel's fortieth anniversary. Edgar Whisenant, in his book, *On Borrowed Time: 88 Reasons Why the Rapture Could Be In 1988*, cited Israel's upcoming birthday as part of "Reason #8" for his prediction.

> God never stopped short of 40 years or days, and God never reached a 41st day or year—therefore the Rapture must occur after Israel's 40th birthday (14 May 1988) and before Israel's 41st birthday (14 May 1989).[4]

On Borrowed Time pegged the rapture as taking place in 1988 during Rosh Hashanah, on either September 11, 12, or 13. "Now we'll just sit down in front of the evening news and watch the events unfold," the book declared. As that date approached more than 3.2 million copies of the book were distributed; by August 1988 it was listed as the second-largest-selling Christian paperback. It could be that many tens of thousands of Christians were eagerly awaiting their departure from earth when the predicted rapture date came and went uneventfully. Stories abound of people who, anticipating the rapture, put their personal affairs in order and said their final goodbyes to unbelieving friends and relatives. *Christianity Today* magazine observed that "columnists, cartoonists, and television newscasters had a heyday."[5]

How could so many Christians become caught up in such an embarrassing goof? One significant reason is that much of contemporary Christendom views the nation of Israel as the centerpiece of what God is doing on earth. This kind of thinking is popular today, but it wasn't always so.

A recent theological emphasis

As part of the research for *The Late Great Planet Earth*, Lindsey looked back several centuries in church history to discover whether noted Christian theologians concurred with the idea that biblical prophecy regarding Israel would be fulfilled by the physical restoration of Palestine. Lindsey examined commentaries dating back to 1611 and found that those who did share his perspective were a minority whose views ran counter to "the prevailing religious opinion of their day."[6]

The fact is that the present emphasis on natural Israel, which in this century has become so prevalent in evangelical, Pentecostal, and charismatic circles, was rejected by many theologians in ages past. From the time of Augustine (A.D. 354 - 430) through that of the great thinkers of the Reformation and on through several more centuries, this obsession with natural Israel was notably absent from the theological mainstream.

Lindsey's method of interpreting prophetic scripture[7] is grounded in a relatively recent development: namely, the advent of dispensationalism, a highly literal method of biblical interpretation introduced primarily by John Darby in the 1830s and later popularized by C.I. Scofield in the early 1900s.

Many Christians today, even without realizing it, are looking at prophecy through a set of "dispensational" eye glasses. Their vision is focused on the Middle East because they are looking for God's promises to be fulfilled in a literal, physical way.

Let me pose this question: Is this way of looking at things biblically justified? Is the exaltation of a natural race of people biblically appropriate?

There is no doubt that God intends for us to have zeal for His nation. But those who have tried to figure out the puzzle of the Bible based on a picture they see with their natural eyes will exalt a people identified by their ancestry, not by their faith. In doing so, they will always meet with frustration and confusion, perhaps even with doubts about the validity of the Word of God.

Let's refer back to our puzzle principles to answer this most important question: Who is the Israel of God?

Puzzle Principle No. 1:
The New Interprets the Old

John the Baptist, Jesus, and the apostle Paul, who all participated in communicating the meaning of the Old Testament, shocked the Jewish leaders of their day with declarations concerning the identity of the true Jews, those who constitute the "Israel of God." Natural lineage, as we have seen, did not rank very high on their list of qualifications. As a matter of fact, it didn't even appear there.

Remembering that Jesus Himself and the New Testament writers had full revelation of the truth, let's look briefly at a few incidents that demonstrate their points of view.

1. The religious leaders during Jesus' days on earth claimed special standing before God because of their natural lineage.

"Abraham is our father," they claimed. "We are his descendants."

Jesus scandalized them with His reply. "If you were Abraham's children, then you would do the things Abraham did"; then, even more bluntly, "You do not belong to God."

Jesus flatly rejected the claim of these men to membership in God's family. He was saying that they, Jews by birth, were not among the descendants God had promised Abraham. They were not part of the offspring who would come through Sarah, who would number as the "stars in the sky," and who would bless all the nations of the earth. Jesus was underscoring the theme that God's family is spiritual, not natural.

2. The apostle Paul said that his natural qualifications as a Jew outweighed anyone's.

> If anyone else thinks he has reasons to put confidence in the flesh, I have more: circumcised on the eighth day, of the people of Israel, of the tribe of Benjamin,

a Hebrew of Hebrews; in regard to the law, a Pharisee; as for zeal, persecuting the church; as for legalistic righteousness, faultless.[8]

Paul once saw all these as valuable credentials. But his perspective had radically changed. He now counted it all "rubbish" in exchange for knowing Christ, that he might have "the righteousness that comes from God and is by faith."[9]

A dangerous threat

Paul's perspective on spiritual matters got him into serious trouble with the religious teachers of his day, who saw his views as a dangerous threat. One day Paul was in the temple when someone identified him as the theological troublemaker. Several men grabbed him and started challenging the content of his preaching. Their words so incensed the crowd that a riot erupted, and a mob began beating Paul with the intent of killing him.

Why was the crowd in such an uproar? "This is the man," they said, "who teaches all men everywhere against our people, the law and this place."[10] Paul, like the other apostles, was going around explaining who the people of God were, what the Law really meant, and what the Temple represented. His words angered the crowd because Paul had a completely different concept of what these things were all about, and his vision left them completely out of the picture. Instead of a nation of natural birth, he saw a spiritual people, joined and knit together in the body of Christ.[11]

Also, instead of viewing the law as a religious rule book, the New Testament writers saw it with spiritual eyes, perceiving that its purpose was to point to the need for salvation from sin. ("The law is only a shadow of the good things that are coming—not the realities themselves," says Hebrews 10:1.)[12] Also, these men didn't view the house of God as an entity in the natural realm, an ancient stone structure in Jerusalem;[13] to them, the house of God was something spiritual, something eternal, a house built with living stones:

> Consequently, you are no longer foreigners and aliens, but fellow citizens with God's people and members of God's household, built on the foundation of the apostles and prophets, with Christ Jesus himself as the chief cornerstone. In him the whole building is joined together and rises to become a holy temple in the Lord. And in him you too are being built together to become a dwelling in which God lives by his Spirit.[14]

That view was reiterated by Peter in his epistles to the churches.[15] The prophetic promises of Scripture about the house of God were not speaking of Old Testament temples; they were pointing toward a spiritual house—the church.

A spiritual interpretation

The Jews interpreted things naturally; Jesus and the apostles interpreted things spiritually. Paul had abandoned his natural thinking, with its emphasis on religious works and national origin, and had been converted to a spiritual vision. He realized that some of Abraham's natural descendants were not true citizens of spiritual Israel. Citizenship in the nation of God was based on a relationship with God by faith, nothing else. Each one of Israel's citizens, from Abraham on down, had the same credentials: they had attained their citizenship by faith.[16] This was the perspective conveyed by the writers of the New Testament.

Puzzle Principle No. 2:
The Mind Set on the Flesh is Death

Applying this second principle helps to further resolve some of the confusion about Israel's true identity. If you conclude that God has placed the natural nation of Israel at the center of His dealings, then you have fixed your mind on matters of the flesh. But that point of view, one based on flesh, is associated with death. Let's look at the story of the birth of this new nation of Israel to help clarify that the Bible is directed toward a spiritual nation.

Abraham and Sarah

God's promise to Abraham of a son seemed to him to take too long in coming. As humans are inclined to do, Sarah developed a more feasible strategy to "help" bring about the promise of God. Her plan provided a convenient way for the "promise" of a child to be brought about—by natural means. "Close enough," Abraham may have thought. "God gave me a brain, so I ought to use it." So with a "surrogate mother"—Sarah's servant Hagar— Abraham fathered a son.

As any natural father would, Abraham felt a strong affection for his first-born son, Ishmael. But despite Abraham's devotion, a problem remained: Ishmael did not represent the promise of God. His life demonstrated what man can do in the flesh, not what God can do by His Spirit.

When God visited Abraham to let him know that Sarah would have a child and be the mother of nations, he fell on his face and laughed at the thought of a 100-year-old man and a ninety-year-old woman bearing a child. Abraham tried his best to persuade God to let Ishmael fill the role of the promised son. "Oh, that Ishmael might live before Thee," he pleaded.[17]

God had a choice: He could abandon His intention and replace His original plan with the one Abraham had developed;

or, despite Abraham's appeals, God could insist that Abraham follow His plan.

What was His decision? How did He answer Abraham's request to substitute the natural plan for the spiritual promise?

"NO!" God said. "NO! NO! FOREVER NO!" God said no to Ishmael, no to the flesh, no to the idea that His family, His nation, would begin from a foundation laid with human hands.

Fourteen years after Ishmael's birth, Sarah indeed conceived and bore a son: Isaac. This was the son God had promised, the son God intended to use to bring about His purposes. This was the miracle child. God said that the descendants who would go to make up the family that He has been assembling throughout history would come through Isaac, through the promise, through the Spirit.[18]

Again, recognizing that the New Testament writers had been given full understanding of the history of Israel and its relevance to God's plan, consider the straightforward explanation Paul gave the Romans. He was trying to sort out once and for all this question that, unfortunately, still troubles us today: "Who is Israel?"

For not all who are descended from Israel are Israel.[19]

In case that is not clear enough, Paul goes on to spell it out even more plainly:

That is, those who are the children of the flesh, these are not the children of God but the children of the promise are regarded as descendants.[20]

Now he has clarified the point that naturally born Jews are not automatically part of Israel. Who is Israel, then? He offers the answer in the same passage:

Through Isaac your descendants will be named.[21]

In other words, it is not the natural children who are God's children, but it is the children of the promise who are regarded as Abraham's offspring.

> Now we, brethren, as Isaac was, are children of promise.[22]

That statement clearly reduces to nothing the significance of natural lineage. The people of God are a miracle people, produced like Isaac.

Our spiritual fathers

I recently listened to a man who was interpreting the Bible according to natural thinking, saying that Israel would be the focal point of the culmination of history. I disagreed with most of what he said, except what he said while praying. While he was praying he kept making these references:
"Abraham, Isaac, and Jacob . . . ."
"Abraham, Isaac, and Jacob . . . ."
"Abraham, Isaac, and Jacob . . . ." His prayer was heavily punctuated with references to the forefathers of Israel. That piqued my interest, and I started wondering. Whose forefathers are these men, anyway? Are they the forefathers of natural Jews, like David Ben-Gurion, Itzhak Shamir, and Golda Meir? Or of spiritual Jews, like C.H. Spurgeon, John Wesley, and Billy Graham?

Let's think about how these three biblical characters came to be the foundation of Israel.

Abraham. When first called by God, Abraham was not a Jew. He was living in a heathen land. God spoke to this man, directing him to leave his family and set out for a different land. After he responded in faith, God spoke again to him and promised that his offspring would be as numerous as the sand on the seashore and the stars in the sky. Abraham was not chosen because of his natural characteristics. He became a Jew supernaturally when God made him one.

Isaac. God promised Abraham that he would have a son, and Abraham and Sarah resorted to natural means to fulfill the promise. But God's purpose was to be accomplished through Isaac, the child born by supernatural means.

Jacob. Jacob's role in Israel also was determined not by natural characteristics but by the promise of God. While Isaac's two children, Jacob and Esau, were in Rebecca's womb, the Lord said to her: "The older will serve the younger."[23]

God disregarded the natural rule. In that society, the firstborn was first in command among the family's siblings. But before Esau and Jacob were born, God made a choice that the younger would be in charge. The children themselves didn't do anything to bring this about. They didn't do anything wrong; they didn't do anything right. They were just born. God intervened in the natural order, further underlining the fact that the foundation of His nation was not one of natural lineage.

Hatred for Esau

The description of God's attitude toward Esau can be one of the most difficult portions of the Bible to understand. On the surface, it seems that God had some harsh things to say about him:

> It is written, "Jacob I have loved, but Esau I have hated."[24]

There's no misprint. The passage actually says that God *hated* Esau! Our inclination is to say that God surely does not mean this, it's not consistent with His character, something must have been lost in the translation, and so on. The most frequent explanation I've heard of this verse says that God hated Esau because he sold his birthright. I personally cannot accept that point of view. The Bible mentions plenty of people, including some of the patriarchs, kings, and apostles, whose behavior at times makes them look like far worse violators than Esau. But God never said He hated any of them. Furthermore, if God hated Esau for what he did, what must He think about you and me?

The fault in this explanation lies in the assumption that we earn God's love. The Bible makes it very clear that God loved us even when we were dead in our transgressions. To understand what the scriptures regarding Esau are communicating, we have to see that God did not hate the man named Esau. That would indeed have been cruel, not at all consistent with the nature of a God who is love. If that were so, we would have to rewrite John 3:16 to say, "For God so loved the world—*except for Esau.*"

The reason for God saying He hated Esau is this: Esau, in the context of biblical history, represents the flesh. He represents the natural; he represents works. He represents the nature of every person who believes that within themselves they can earn right standing with God.

The Bible says that no flesh shall glory in God's presence,[25] that flesh and blood shall not inherit the kingdom of God,[26] and that the just shall live by faith, not by works.[27] God wants to get it into our minds that Israel is spiritual, not natural, that Israel is a miracle. God's activities are motivated by grace, not by works, not by natural considerations. His dealings with men have always been according to His grace.

The forefathers of Israel gained their status in God's nation supernaturally. Their roles were the result of God's work, not their own. Likewise, those who are born supernaturally, through rebirth in Christ, become part of God's family. Natural birth is no guarantee. Spiritual birth is the only means of entry into God's nation.

That is what Paul tried to explain to the Jews, and that is why they had him flogged. Paul listed his religious credentials and said each of the items was worthless since true Judaism is a matter of the heart. Jesus was trying to get this same message across to Nicodemus and the Pharisees and Sadducees. They were getting tripped up by their natural thinking, but Jesus kept pointing to the spiritual dimension.

Puzzle Principle No. 3:
Shadow Leads to Substance

This third principle helped bring a perspective on elements of the Old Testament that had kept me confused for years. Not that I understood them suddenly; but as I read back through some key Old Testament passages, I ended up inspired, eager to consider a passage's implications for the present and future, rather than bewildered by its apparent lack of relevance to our day.

The shadow-and-substance principle addresses a key question about God's purposes: When did God devise the plan to focus His attention on a spiritual people? Was this His idea from the beginning? Or did He switch gears and introduce a new, more spiritual approach once Jesus came to earth? This principle helped me see the continuity of God's dealings with men throughout history, as recorded in the Bible. Partially because of a new understanding about shadows and substance, I've ended up with the conviction that the entire Bible is indeed directed toward a spiritual people referred to as Israel, not toward the natural nation of the same name.

It may be easy for you to agree that the New Testament makes a clear distinction between the flesh and the spirit. You may be wondering, though, whether the same distinction applied back in the days of Noah, Abraham, Moses, and David.

Again, from the explanations given by Jesus and the writers of the New Testament, it is clear that from the beginning God has focused His efforts on His spiritual family. The natural nation of Israel, which God used to demonstrate His character and communicate His purpose, was merely a shadow pointing to its spiritual counterpart. That counterpart is unveiled in the New Testament as the church.

The implications of this concept are enormous. We'll consider them later, but first let's look at some scriptures that deal with the time frame of God's focus on a spiritual people.

When Jesus said, "I will build my church and the gates of hell will not prevail against it," He was not announcing a new plan; He was only disclosing more information about the plan He had had from the beginning.[28] Paul said that part of his calling was to unravel that mystery, which had "been hidden in ages past." This is what he said God revealed to him:

> His [God's] intent was that now, *through the church,* the manifold wisdom of God should be made known to the rulers and authorities in the heavenly realms, *according to his eternal purpose which he accomplished in Christ Jesus.*[29] [author's italics]

The church's role

The apostle's task was to disclose the "secret" that the church is at the center of the *eternal* purpose of God. Scripture says that through the redeeming power of Jesus, God would create a spiritual people who would bring His light into a fallen world. That was God's design from the beginning. There was no other plan, no other hope. God, in a profound miracle that we cannot fully understand, chooses to supernaturally dwell within a flawed and frail people, and through them display His glory to mankind. That is the same mystery of which Paul wrote in Colossians:

> To them [the saints] God has chosen to make known among the Gentiles the glorious riches of this mystery, which is Christ in you, the hope of glory.[30]

The Greek word *you* in this passage is plural: Christ in *you all*—that is, Christ in all of us together. One by one, we can't begin to reflect the majesty of God. But God has determined to have a *people,* a spiritual nation spanning all continents and cultures, to be a showcase of His splendor.[31]

Israel was used in God's plan, but like the law it was imperfect, unable to accomplish God's ultimate purpose. That nation was the shadow of something better, something that was not fully disclosed until Jesus came.

When the New Testament writers were given revelation on God's purpose, they looked back with new perception on what happened in the Old Testament. They saw the spiritual significance of what God had done in the natural realm. They saw the manna in the wilderness pointing to the Bread of Life, and the Levitical priesthood pointing to the One who would be High Priest forever. They saw the temple in Jerusalem pointing to a people built together as a spiritual house, a holy temple in which God lives by His Spirit. And they saw that the Hebrew nation pointed to something of far greater significance: a spiritual people.

The New Testament writers weren't announcing a revision of the divine plan. All along, the Lord has sought a spiritual people, a people who trusted in Him alone for their salvation. It wouldn't matter if one were born hundreds of years before Christ or hundreds of years after; it wouldn't matter if one came from the Middle East or the American Midwest. What matters is faith. God "will justify the circumcised [natural Jews] by faith and the uncircumcised [Gentiles] through that same faith."[32] Faith is the only door into the kingdom of heaven. It always has been, and it always will be.

For there is no distinction between Jew and Greek, for the same Lord over all is rich to all who call upon Him. For "whoever calls upon the name of the Lord shall be saved."[33]

A single plan

God does not have two plans: one accomplished by natural means and the other by the Spirit. God does not have two peoples: one conceived in the flesh, and the other in the Spirit. He has one people. God loves natural Jews, just as He loves spiritual Jews, but He does not have a separate plan for them. There is only one way natural Jews can become citizens in the Israel of God. It is the same salvation strategy—"by grace through faith"—that everyone must follow.

After covering this theological ground, what answer would you give to the question, "Who is Israel?" Would you now say that Israel comprises those who, through the ages, have trusted in God for their salvation? If so, you can then draw the conclusion that as believers in Jesus we are the "children of the promise," Abraham's true descendants. You will then see these believers as God's family, the members of His household, the chosen people, the royal priesthood, the one great nation God has created to fulfill His great purpose.

This understanding of the church as the true Israel of God leads to a startling conclusion: *the church will be that company of people who will ultimately receive the fulfillment of all of God's promises to Israel.*

CHAPTER
9

THE PROMISES

A few years ago I was in Italy to minister at a leaders' conference being held at a church in a small city called Caserta, not far from Naples. During my stay I took a trip to the Isle of Capri with some people from the church. While boarding the boat a man in front of me slipped, and I caught him just in time to keep him from taking a sudden side trip into the Mediterranean. He and his wife thanked me, and we started talking. One of my Italian friends, Salvatore, mentioned that I was a pastor and would be speaking at his church.

It turned out that these other tourists, like myself, were from New York City. We talked about the city a while; then I directed the conversation onto a different subject.

"Are you Catholic?" I asked. I figured that since they were from New York and were visiting Italy, there was a good chance they were. "You know," I said, "this is a great place for Catholics to visit."

"No, we're Jewish," the man said.

Before I even had a chance to think about what I was saying, I responded: "Oh, really? Me, too."

"You are?" he asked, looking puzzled.

They just stared for a minute. I could tell the wheels were spinning. A pastor? Jewish? That didn't compute. They were thinking I was joking or that perhaps I had a Jewish mother. The man smiled and repeated his question, waiting for me to show what I had up my sleeve.

"So you're Jewish, huh?" he said.

"Yes, I am," I replied, smiling pleasantly.

He decided to go over things one more time. "You said you were a pastor?"

"That's right."

"Your name is Tosini?"

"Right."

It took a minute for them to recover from the shock of this Christian pastor claiming to be a Jew. Then the man decided he would give me a little quiz to test my Jewishness. Each time I answered one of his questions, his wife would say in her strong New York "Jewish mother" tone, "That's terrific!"

Finally he said, "If you're really a Jew, complete this statement: 'If I forget you, O . . . .'"

Fortunately I had been teaching on that psalm recently and could quickly quote the rest of the passage. "If I forget you, O Jerusalem, may my right hand forget its skill. May my tongue cling to the roof of my mouth if I don't exalt Jerusalem above my highest joy. Psalm 137."

The man was extremely surprised, for I not only knew the scripture, but I recited it with such deep conviction that I convinced him of my genuine belief in that passage.

"Okay. Now it's my turn," I said, ready to demonstrate which one of us was the real Jew. "Question number one: How many children did Abraham have?"

"Two," he said. "But Isaac was the main one." Actually he had several more, but I did not think it was important to correct him.

"Okay," I said. "Question number two: How old was Sarah when Isaac was born?"

"Ninety," he responded, pleased with himself for knowing the answer.

"Right," I said. "So, how did a ninety-year-old woman have a child?" He leaned forward, looked me right in the eye, and said boldly, "Isaac was a miracle."

I leaned forward, looked him right back in the eye and said: "So am I, and there isn't a real Jew who isn't." I waited a moment for that to sink in. Then I pulled my last punch: "Are you a miracle?"

The miracle message

I could see that the message made sense to him. This man's standing as a Jew was based on who his natural parents were. That's no miracle; it's natural lineage. My standing as a Jew, on the other hand, is based on the miracle God did in my heart when I accepted Jesus. That was the moment at which God made me an heir to the promise, a fellow heir with all others who have believed God.

An anti-semitic message?

The world has been plagued for centuries by antagonism, even unbridled cruelty, toward Jewish people. This historical bigotry culminated in our own era with the emergence of a demented leader in Germany. Everyone, Christian and non-Christian alike, should be horrified by the hatred directed toward the Jews in the past, and by the bigotry that continues to surface.

As I have spoken with people about the identity of the Israel of the Bible, my theological statements have at times been misapplied. While making the theological point that the biblical promises directed to Israel are intended for the church, some people have incorrectly concluded that I am somehow opposed to the nation of Israel and its citizens. That is not the case. Jewish people have standing in God's eyes equal to that of any other race. They are no better, no worse; they are simply people who, like the rest of us, need Jesus.

As people with sensitivity to uprightness and justice, our emotional inclination is often to support the political interests of the modern nation of Israel because of the Jews' painful history. But it would be inappropriate to likewise allow our theological conclusions to be affected by our emotional outrage over the horrible crimes committed against these people.

Many Christians add to the theological confusion about the spiritual condition of Jews. An attitude that provides special spiritual status to Jews leads to some subtle but significant problems for believers. For example, when we refer to Jews who accept Christ as "completed Jews," we imply that they had a head start because of their natural heritage. The implication is that while I, as a Gentile, needed to be "converted" from a depraved, sinful lifestyle, a Jew needs only to be "completed."

It is a subtle point, but this viewpoint has had a dramatic impact on the mentality of modern Christians. One prominent leader with a national following once said that every time he meets a Jewish person he listens carefully to what the person says. Why? Because Jews have a "prophetic instinct," he said. Where does this idea come from? Where is this man placing his confidence–in the flesh or in the spirit?

Christians, of course, feel a special regard for the "Holy Land," because it's the land of Jesus' birth and the setting for much of what happened in the Bible. But interest often goes beyond simple curiosity about historic sites in the Bible; people often see the country as somehow having a special spiritual climate. One television show on a Christian broadcasting network featured an Israeli tourism official.

"Come to Israel," he told viewers. "You can pray in your church every day, but there is no place on earth where you can feel as close to God as in Israel. This is the Holy Land." The show's host heartily agreed.

That troubled me. A leader in the Christian community was agreeing with an unbeliever who said that the presence of God in the church would always be inferior to God's presence in a particular geographic location. What did Jesus mean in His response to the Samaritan woman, who was confused about God's desired location for worship? "The Jews," she said, "tell us that Jerusalem is the place to worship. Our fathers say Samaria is the place to worship." Jesus said they were both wrong, and told her that God is looking for people who will worship Him in spirit and truth.

Is that true? Does God have a special presence in Jerusalem today? Is Jerusalem a holier city than, say, Albuquerque, Seattle, or London?

Are Israel's citizens, at least those of Jewish descent, objects of special grace and somehow different from Europeans or Asians or Africans?

The answers depend on whether you are looking at Israel from a natural or a spiritual viewpoint. God said that the natural city of Jerusalem corresponds to Hagar, who birthed a son according to the flesh.[1] The truth about the Israel of God and the spiritual status of natural Jews was hard for believers to grasp in the first century A.D., and obviously we are still wrestling with it.

However apparent this truth might seem to some people, it remains the cause of widespread confusion today. One large-circulation Christian magazine, for example, featured a cover story on the believers in Israel. The article noted that "Jewish believers take great pains to emphasize that despite their commitment to Jesus they are not 'Christians,' " and it described a burgeoning movement in which Jewish believers prefer to meet in their own assemblies to distinguish themselves from other followers of Christ. The magazine quoted a woman from Tel Aviv, who said, "Because a Jew believes in the Messiah does not make him a Gentile." She continued:

> It is not right for a Jew to be saved, then disappear into the church. That is not even biblical. The Jews are to be grafted back into the olive tree, not all the different vines.[2]

Prophetic focus

Christians who fix their attention on Israel tend, while reading the Bible, to use current events for clues to the problem of figuring out how God is going to use that country in His divine plan. Such people just get confused. They end up speculating on how the latest terrorist act or military clash figures in the end-times scenario. This diverts attention from what God wants to accomplish through His church.

Natural thinking has a way of clouding our vision so that we do not see the picture God sees. To sharpen our spiritual vision it should help to take a look at several prophetic passages in Scripture referring to Israel's role in the future. As you read, think of these passages as referring not to a natural nation, but to a spiritual nation of which you, if you are a Christian, are a part.

These are some of the most thrilling passages of the Bible. If you read them with the understanding that the Old Testament promises directed to Israel still apply to the people of God, the church, you will see that we have a wonderful, powerful future ahead of us.

Applying the prophetic promises of the Old Testament to the church might be new for you, something that causes you to reexamine beliefs you have always held. It's important to sort out this issue, though, because we're not talking about some irrelevant theological point, like how many angels can dance on the head of a pin. We are talking about whether a huge portion of the Bible is relevant to Christians and their future or whether it is talking about another group of people altogether.

The prophets' audience

The first issue to clarify as we look at prophetic scriptures is this: Who were the prophets talking about when they foretold what would happen to Israel? Were they prophesying for a people who would inherit these promises due to their ethnic heritage, or were they speaking to a people who would be heirs because of their spiritual birth?

First Peter 1:10-12 helps answer this question:

> Concerning this salvation, the prophets, who spoke of
> the grace that was to come to you, searched intently

and with the greatest care, trying to find out the time and circumstances to which the Spirit of Christ in them was pointing when he predicted the sufferings of Christ and the glories that would follow. It was revealed to them that they were not serving themselves but you, when they spoke of the things that have now been told you by those who have preached the gospel to you by the Holy Spirit.

This passage says that the Old Testament prophets were delivering their message *to the church*.

The promises

Now let's take a look at a few of these promises and hear what God is saying to the church. Read, for example, this passage in Isaiah:

Arise, shine; for your light has come! And the glory of the Lord is risen upon you. For behold, the darkness shall cover the earth, and deep darkness the people; but the Lord will arise over you, and His glory will be seen upon you. The Gentiles shall come to your light, and kings to the brightness of your rising.

Lift up your eyes all around, and see: they all gather together, they come to you; your sons shall come from afar, and your daughters shall be nursed at your side. Then you shall see and become radiant, and your heart shall swell with joy; because the abundance of the sea shall be turned to you, the wealth of the Gentiles shall come to you. . . . And I will glorify the house of My glory.[3]

Upon whom will the glory of the Lord rise and be seen? To whose light will the nations come, and who will be the recipients of the Gentiles' wealth? What is the house of God's glory? Will a natural or a spiritual people be a radiant light to the Gentiles?

A message to the church

Understanding that the Old Testament prophets were ultimately speaking to the church makes the Bible a far more exciting and relevant book for believers today. Consider the implications of these promises:

> He [the Lord] has declared that he will set you in praise, fame and honor high above all the nations he has made and that you will be a people holy to the Lord your God, as he promised.[4]

> David said, . . . "the house to be built for the Lord should be of great magnificence and fame and splendor in the sight of all the nations." [5]

> In that day this song will be sung in the land of Judah: We have a strong city; God makes salvation its walls and ramparts. Open the gates that the righteous nation may enter, the nation that keeps faith. [6]

> The sons of your oppressors will come bowing before you; all who despise you will bow down at your feet and will call you The City of the Lord, Zion of the Holy One of Israel. Although you have been forsaken and hated, with no one traveling through, I will make you the everlasting pride and the joy of all generations. [7]

> You will call your walls Salvation and your gates Praise. . . . The Lord will be your everlasting light . . . .Then will all your people be righteous and they will possess the land forever. [8]

> The nations will see your righteousness, and all kings your glory; you will be called by a new name that the

mouth of the Lord will bestow. You will be a crown of splendor in the Lord's hand, a royal diadem. [9]

This is what the Lord Almighty says: "In those days ten men from all languages and nations will take firm hold of one Jew by the edge of his robe and say, 'Let us go with you, because we have heard that God is with you.'" [10]

The Lord their God will save them on that day as the flock of his people. They will sparkle in his land like jewels in a crown. How attractive and beautiful they will be! [11]

In the last days the mountain of the Lord's temple will be established as chief among the mountains; it will be raised above the hills, and peoples will stream to it. Many nations will come and say, "Come, let us go up to the mountain of the Lord, to the house of the God of Jacob. He will teach us his ways, so that we may walk in his paths." [12]

Did you catch some of those descriptions of what the church is destined to become? Not a reproach, but an everlasting pride and joy. A sparkling jewel. A people of renown. The church will be held in high honor, and people will stream to it because they can see God at work in its midst.

Passages like these, declaring the high destiny of God's people, are scattered throughout the Old Testament. The promises are given to those who are the spiritual descendants of Abraham, those who belong to the household of faith. Unfortunately, many believers have the mentality that natural Israel will fulfill these promises. Because of that outlook, they can not accept that these promises will be fulfilled in the body of Christ, the church.

Roots in Abraham

Although an American by natural birth, I am a spiritual Israelite with my roots in Abraham, part of a nation that has been created and called by God to give hope to a hopelessly failing human community. I am not looking for another people to respond to Isaiah's call to "arise, shine," because he was saying that God's glorious light would shine in *us,* in followers of Christ. That is the mystery the New Testament writers revealed: Christ in us—His church—the hope of glory. The Spirit of Christ abides in His people.

The Old Testament becomes fascinating when you understand that it's a letter written to us. The letter says, "Keep your eyes on God's people because He has some incredible plans for them." My eyes are not fixed on current events in the Middle East. Instead, they are focused on the nation of God and its certain destiny:

> Whereas you have been forsaken and hated, so that no one went through you, I will make you an eternal excellence, a joy of many generations.[13]

This has been God's fixed purpose for Israel—spiritual Israel—from before the foundation of the world. And, as the Lord declared in Scripture, "Indeed I have spoken it; I will also bring it to pass. I have purposed it; I will also do it."[14]

If you adopt the point of view that you are part of that nation destined to become an eternal excellence, you will undergo some dramatic changes. It will change the way you think, the things you do, the way you spend your money. It will cause you to realize that your life is of great significance.

CHAPTER 10

VISION

Great leaders possess great vision—the ability to climb high above the demands of the present to imagine a future not yet realized. Corporate executives are employing vision when they plan ten, twenty, or thirty years into the future. I've heard of business leaders who chart their organization's future into the next generation, setting goals that extend past their own lifetimes. One particularly visionary Japanese executive reportedly has drawn up plans outlining the direction his company will take for the next hundred years.

Secular leaders recognize how essential foresight is to a prosperous future. As Christians, especially those who are leaders, our vision cannot be out of focus or we will wander from one cause to another, from one popular trend to the next, without a clear sense of where we are supposed to end up.

The roadmap

As believers, we need the direction and inspiration that a vision provides. We can't afford to wander aimlessly through the Christian life; we need a roadmap clearly marked with our destination. If someone doesn't know where he's going, he might be headed for disaster. "Where there is no vision,"

Proverbs says, "the people perish."[1] The *New American Standard Bible* translation says, "Where there is no vision, the people are unrestrained."

Treasures in the sand

The confusion about Israel helps explain the significance of vision. If the same devotion, hope, and confidence of success Christians have in Israel were directed toward the church, the world would see the light and salt Jesus promised. The church's mentality would match the prophetic promises God gave her; and, as it says in Romans, the Jewish people and the nation of Israel would be made envious, leading them to acknowledge Jesus as the true Messiah.[2]

As we look at the subject of Israel as an example of misdirected vision, keep in mind that this is not a political opinion. It is a spiritual statement identifying the church as the nation of God's desire, the apple of His eye, the city on a hill that men must see in order for Jesus to be glorified. Unfortunately, a misplaced emphasis will put our confidence in the flesh, not in the spirit. The result: weak, ill-equipped Christians floundering through a maze of futility.

A front-page article in *The Wall Street Journal* told of several Christian oil men who have invested huge sums in Israel in hopes of finding the world's largest petroleum deposit.[3] Their search was inspired by the prophecy in Deuteronomy 33. The passage says that the land given Zebulun and Issachar would have "treasures hidden in the sand" and that Asher would "bathe his feet in oil."

The prospect of a massive oil field lying beneath Israel ignited hopes that the financial boom resulting from such a find would fulfill the prophecy that Israel would be "blessed above nations" and would usher in the Second Coming. One organizer said the discovery would rank as the "most significant event in history."

Several drilling firms set out on multimillion-dollar oil

exploration projects, including one $20 million venture, and turned to evangelical leaders for the money. Fund-raising appeals were aired on national television, and one prominent television evangelist told his viewers that the project "could revolutionize the fulfillment of Bible prophecy." A book titled *The Great Treasure Hunt* was sold at revival meetings and bookstores, and Christian radio stations swept up in the excitement broadcast updates on the drillers' progress.

Busloads of believers flocked to the wells to fast and pray, and when news came of an impending gusher, Americans chartered planes to Israel so they would be on hand for the historic occasion. But euphoria over the well dissipated, when, at 20,500 feet below the surface, drillers abandoned the dry hole.

Zeal for Israel lies behind it all. Yet despite huge investments and enormous enthusiasm for the project, no one has struck oil there. One Denver oilman spent $3.5 million drilling on Mount Carmel before he ran out of money. Atop the mountain, he had flown a giant flag that read, "God loves Israel and I do too."

One 76-year-old widow told the newspaper she had borrowed $2,000 to "bless Israel." She prays night and day for a gusher because "oil will anoint the chosen people and they'll become believers" in Jesus.

These are people with an intense passion for Israel; their devotion fuels a fierce determination to see the prophecies given to Israel become a reality. Their cause has cost them a great deal, but has not yielded fulfillment. As one pastor summed up the result of such pursuits, "it left us all with an empty feeling."

A grievous error

A few years ago, a prominent Christian organization published a magazine with a cover story about how Israel had developed an export market for its oranges. The cover photo featured a closeup of these oranges, which were being sold in Europe. Oranges received all this attention because the magazine was saying they represented the fulfillment of Isaiah 27:6:

> In the days to come Jacob will take root, Israel will bud
> and blossom and fill all the world with fruit.

Is this what God wants us to get excited about—Israeli oranges? Drilling rigs in Palestine? At some point we will have to stop and recognize that a grievous error has been made: that of filtering the biblical promises to Israel through natural logic rather than through spiritual wisdom. The natural nation of Israel, the natural city of Jerusalem, and the natural Temple of Solomon are real enough. But they merely point to a spiritual reality of far greater significance, one in which Christ reigns over and through a people of faith. We have been waiting for God to shower blessings of peace, security, joy, and prosperity upon a natural people. Our wait is in vain. People of natural birth may export natural fruit, but the fruit that God intends to export can only be produced by a people of supernatural birth.

The local church investment

The Father's deepest passion is for the children of the promise. When God says we should invest in Israel, He is talking about an investment in the church. He's saying to put your money, your time, your energy, your devotion, into the spiritual house of God. Only God's people, in whom His Spirit dwells, can produce the dividends of the kingdom: righteousness, peace, and joy.

Your wisest investment will be to devote yourself to the spiritual well-being of the believers around you in your local church. Make it your passion to see the promises of God come true in their lives; dedicate yourself to that cause. Pray that these people will prosper. Be determined that they will become a people of renown, joy, praise, and honor. Devote yourself to them, and you will begin to see Israel blossom before your eyes. You will see fruit, imperishable fruit, and you will find "treasures hidden in the sand."

Perhaps that's difficult for you to imagine when you think of your church. When you look at the people sitting around you, the promises of abundance and renown may seem far off.

If we look at outward circumstances, we will always come away saying, "There's no way that God's promises will ever be fulfilled in these people." But remember: God gave us these promises. They are based on His ability, not man's. God will build His church. He just wants us to believe what He has promised to do and make ourselves available to do the work He has for us in the church.

As difficult as this will be for some, we need to refocus the vision for Israel. We need to take that same zeal, that same commitment, and direct it toward the church, toward local churches across the world.

Confidence toward Israel, doubts about the church

The emphasis placed on Israel and the end-times scenarios put forth in the last few decades are based on a theology that expects little from the church. I have seen within people a strange fatalism toward the church's future, compared with their confident assurance that no matter what happens Israel will always come out on top. Some seem to display unlimited patience with Israel in contrast with how quickly they write off the church as a lost cause. Fueling this perspective is a teaching about the dark times in which we are living, claiming that the age of grace is drawing to a close and that the antichrist is alive and preparing for his takeover.

About a month after my conversion, when I was still completely ignorant of the Bible, I was invited to a church. The people there displayed heartfelt enthusiasm for the Lord. They worshiped with intensity and were vocal in their response to the preaching. The message that evening was on Noah and the flood; the pastor's point was that "as it was in the days of Noah, so shall it be when Jesus returns."

"Remember, only eight were saved in Noah's day," he told the crowd soberly. "There isn't anything in the Bible that says there will be any more people saved when Jesus comes."

My mouth dropped. I looked around me. There were almost 200 people in that sanctuary, and most of them were saying, "Amen." I thought to myself, "Only eight of us will make it? That's rough. It's going to be hard to stay in God's good graces. No wonder people are asking for prayer and are just trying to hold on until Jesus returns."

On the other hand, these same people had complete confidence that Israel would never be defeated by its enemies in the Middle East. After all, God was with them; Israel was the apple of His eye. He would never break the convenant He had made with them through Abraham. People thought it was wise to stand behind the nation of Israel because that would result in blessing coming to the church. I've heard this many times since. A few years ago, in fact, one prominent Bible teacher said the church would be judged on how it blesses Israel.

While the expectation of increasing weakness and ultimate failure for the church has become the prevailing expectation of our generation, let me pose an important question: Is this the future depicted in the Bible? Is failure what the Bible predicts for God's nation? Dominant voices today say yes. The dominant voices throughout the preceding centuries of Christian history have said no.

The modern prediction of defeat produces a bunker mentality in which people stay crouched down in their foxholes, expecting the worst. Christians feel desperate about "getting people saved," and their anticipation of disaster can stimulate their evangelistic efforts. But this conviction simply motivates them to get as many people as possible into the bunker with them, to save them from eternal destruction. There is no inclination to charge out of the bunker, launch a counterattack, push back the enemy, and reclaim conquered territory. Why? Because according to this view, no matter how powerful an assault the church might be able to launch, its ultimate defeat is predetermined.

Simple logic tells us that this vision becomes a self-fulfilling prophecy. Since no one is motivated to pursue building a strong church, no strong church emerges.

Jesus' vision

It's clear that we have today two very different ways of looking at the future. Many present-day leaders expect the church to grow in stature; they believe that no matter what the future holds, the church will ultimately prevail as a powerful body of committed believers. Others anticipate ongoing decay in the church and ultimate failure. So how do we determine who is right?

Let's look at some of the statements Jesus made to His disciples as He prepared them for a future on earth without Him. One of His comments in particular should shed light on the matter at hand:

> I will build my church, and the gates of hell will not overcome it.[4]

Jesus states clearly that the church is going to stand up against any opposition. Satan will unleash all his power to defeat the church, but the nation of God will prevail. God has destined it to be so; nothing will stand in the way of it coming to pass:

> I am the Lord, the God of all mankind. Is anything too hard for me?[5]

These promises do not mean that political maneuvering and economic dominance are the strategy prescribed for the church to reach its position of preeminence. They simply state the fact that the church will fulfill its God-given destiny.

What future do you see?

Do you have a hope of victory or an expectation of defeat for the church? Are you looking for restoration in the church or disintegration? When you look to the future, are you looking for God to reveal His glory through a spiritual people of which you are a part, or do you see the fulfillment of God's plan coming through a nation in the Middle East? Your perspective makes a big difference because it determines the direction of your Christian life. If your mind is focused on a spiritual nation, you will direct your energies toward the church.

When we talk about vision, we're simply talking about what is in God's heart. From the very beginning God has determined to create for Himself a spiritual family on earth, through whom He would reveal Himself, and through whom His character, heart, and desires would be clearly seen. It is the church's responsibility to literally put on display all that God is. No individual could take on that assignment, but God's living organism, the church, has been issued the assignment of showing forth His glory. When people take hold of that vision, they get excited about being part of the church.

Our generation's confusion

Our generation has clung to a vision of a defeated church. This teaching has so saturated contemporary Christianity that many believers are even unaware of any other outlook. When they hear about a vision of a victorious church, they assume it's something new. But this isn't some theological twist conjured up by a twentieth-century Don Quixote; it's not wishful thinking, nor is it a "think-positive-and-everything-will-turn-out-fine" brand of Christianity. Neither is it an unscriptural outlook on the ascendancy of man formulated by one who does not accept the doctrine of scriptural inerrancy.

Historically, the emphasis on a triumphant church is mainstream, orthodox, biblical Christianity. This doctrine was reaffirmed in the Protestant Reformation, the greatest spiritual renewal within the church in modern history. In the centuries that followed, believers anticipated that God would again visit nations and bring revival, as in fact He did in outpourings such as America's "Great Awakening" in the 1740s. They believed that God would raise the church to greater heights, and that He would continually expand His kingdom worldwide. This gave rise to a sense of purpose based on their confidence in a destiny sure to be fulfilled. That thought dominated Christian consciousness through the nineteenth century. This outlook, full of faith and hope, is evident in the writings of such respected leaders as Charles Spurgeon, Jonathan Edwards, William Carey, George Whitefield, and John Bunyan.

More than a century ago, for example, Spurgeon spoke out against the dampening effect of misapplied prophecy:

> David was not a believer in the theory that the world will grow worse and worse, and that the dispensation will wind up with general darkness, and idolatry. Earth's sun is to go down amid tenfold night if some of our prophetic brethren are to be believed. Not so do we expect, but we look for a day when the dwellers in all lands shall learn righteousness, shall trust in the Savior, shall worship thee alone, O God, "and shall glorify thy name."[6]

Embracing a theology of victory ignites faith to believe that God will bring the church into a far greater dimension of spiritual life and maturity. It produces hope to believe for an outpouring of the Spirit upon us, as was promised in Joel 2.[7] This hope will inspire us to believe that God has good things in store for His people.

The Puritans, for example, also saw the church as an increasingly powerful force:

> The Puritans saw the church as a divine institution, sufficient by God's blessing for the full realization in history of the promise that Christ "shall have dominion also from sea to sea, and from the river unto the ends of the earth" (Psa. 72:8). If the Church is the God-appointed means for the advancement of the kingdom, then her future is beyond all doubt.[8]

History credits the Puritans with altering the moral and spiritual climate of the English-speaking world. One nineteenth-century commentator gave this assessment of the impact of these "men of hope":

> The Puritans, as a body, have done more to elevate the national character than any class of Englishman that ever lived. The source of this influence was their theology, and within that theology there was an attitude to history and to the world which distinguished them as men of hope. In their own day this hope came to expression in pulpits and in books, in Parliaments and upon battlefields, but it did not end there. The outlook they had done so much to inspire went on for nearly two hundred years after their own age and its results were manifold. It colored the spiritual thought of the American colonies; it taught men to expect great outpourings of the Holy Spirit; it prepared the way to the new age of world-missions; and it contributed largely to that sense of destiny which came to characterize the English-speaking Protestant nations.[9]

Words like defeat and dominion, which were terms the Puritans addressed, can set off theological alarms. I am not necessarily promoting Puritan eschatology. I think it is a mistake to adopt rigid, dogmatic positions on biblically ambiguous issues, because it takes us beyond faith into a realm where only answers will satisfy. For example, the Arminians and Calvinists will argue until Jesus comes over the free will of man versus the sovereignty of God. Yet both of those positions find scriptural support. Does man have free will? Yes, he does. Is God sovereign? Yes, He is. Can I explain how these truths can coexist? No, I cannot. Our calling in this life is to walk humbly before God as a people of faith, not to ascertain all the answers to the mysteries of God.

Setting aside the theological debates, just think of what would happen if our generation embraced the vision that inspired the Puritans, praying fervently that God would mightily restore the church in our generation. Imagine the difference it would make if every believer today became convinced that the church—and, yes, even his own local church—has a key role to play as history unfolds.

Michaelangelo, before he would even touch a piece of marble, demanded of himself that he have a vision of what he would create. He would then chisel away everything that didn't belong. We must possess a vision that will enable us to chisel away the mistaken doctrines of the past, eliminate from our ranks loyalty to men's opinions over scripture, and place above all commitment to and confidence in the success of the local church.

SECTION THREE:

THE BARRIERS

CHAPTER 11

THE
PRICE TAG

P receding chapters describe the masterpiece God has painted. His brush strokes have formed a beautiful picture, one which He envisioned before Creation. The picture is a simple one, a family portrait of a people called Israel, yet its implications are profound.

God's family is a nation of faith. God decreed that because of his obedience, Abraham would become the patriarch of a tribe spanning cultures and centuries, a family destined to bless every nation on earth. It is through this family—created, inhabited, and sustained by the Holy Spirit—that God has chosen to reveal Himself.

Begun by a miracle of faith, the family has a heritage of men and women who have lived by faith. It is a lineage of champions: people of all ages, races, and countries who have run the race, fought the fight, and finished the course. These are the saints who inhabit the "Jerusalem above," the city without foundations whose builder and maker is God.[1] These are Abraham's children—as many as the stars in the sky and the sand on the seashore. Among our number are the cloud of witnesses the writer of Hebrews describes: people such as Abraham, Isaac, and Jacob; Ruth and Rahab; Gideon and David. Our family is formed of God's people in the Old Testament and the New, the great saints of the church like Augustine, Francis Assisi, Luther, Calvin, and Wesley, and on down to the believers in your own local church.

As this picture takes shape in your mind, the purpose of God comes into clearer focus. Can you see its exquisite artistry, its grand design, its compelling beauty? This miracle, given through God's grace, is a divine masterpiece.

You have probably thought that this picture doesn't seem consistent with the picture of the church today. If an artist were to put brush to canvas with the church of today as his subject, what would his picture look like? Perhaps observers would look at the finished canvas and remark, "Is this what's supposed to be the joy of many generations and an eternal excellence? Are you *sure?*"

Their comments on the church might include adjectives like "feeble," "impotent," and "irrelevant," if not worse. And, frankly, if you look around the present landscape, it's not hard to understand why.

Failure in the church

The church's reputation has been soiled by self-appointed and self-serving leaders. Some have fallen victim to the entanglements of sin and pride that can beset people in positions of influence. Others have floundered because they are misplaced in the body of Christ.

In other situations, what some try to pass off as the church of God is only a museum of fossilized religious traditions and empty rituals. Elsewhere, entire denominations have rejected biblical authority, becoming quasi-religious sanctuaries where unsaved people are sheltered from the transforming power of the gospel.

So what do we do now: Sink with despair and quit? Join the throngs who have given up on the church? Try to strike out on our own and paint a different but incomplete picture of God's purpose? Those responses are tempting, but investing in something other than God's original picture will result in even more disappointment, more frustration, more futility.

Remember that God is not showing us the picture of His purpose for our entertainment. This painting poses a choice: *to be part of it or be apart from it.* The decision is not easy. It requires careful consideration, because becoming part of the picture requires the ultimate investment.

The story of two seekers

Some of the toughest passages in the Bible are those in which Jesus talks about the cost of following Him.

John 12 relates a story about two Greeks who were in Jerusalem for the Passover feast. Word about Jesus had reached them, and these two men were interested. They wanted to meet Jesus in person, so they approached Philip, one of His disciples, and asked if he could get them an audience with the teacher from Nazareth.

That seemed like a fine idea to Philip. The men were foreigners and had traveled a long way to get to Jerusalem for the Passover, but they weren't satisfied just with their sojourn in the City of David. They wanted something more. Philip must have thought to himself, "How wonderful! Two hungry seekers with a lot of questions. They want to know Jesus. I wish more people like these would come around."

Philip grabbed Andrew, told him about the two men, and the disciples went to tell Jesus. You can imagine what Philip might have said: "These two men have come a long way to see You. They're ready to join us."

Jesus didn't respond by chatting with the Greek men and making them feel at ease. He began talking about the cost of discipleship.

I tell you the truth, unless a kernel of wheat falls to the ground and dies, it remains only a single seed. But if it dies, it produces many seeds. The man who loves his life will lose it, while the man who hates his life in this world will keep it for eternal life.[2]

Imagine Philip's dismay. "How will these men ever want to join us if Jesus keeps telling them they're going to have to die?"

Jesus continued by saying, "If anyone serves me, let him follow me." Follow Him? Where was Jesus going? He would soon tell the disciples His destination. He was on His way to be crucified.

How can we draw near to Jesus? How can we know Him and learn how to follow Him? *Jesus says we can share in His life by sharing in His death.* He said it clearly and repeatedly:

> Anyone who does not take his cross and follow me is not worthy of me.[3]

> If anyone would come after me, he must deny himself and take up his cross and follow me.[4]

> Anyone who does not carry his cross and follow me cannot be my disciple.[5]

Jesus said He came to give us life in abundance. All you have to do to receive it, He said, is to be crucified. This is somewhat confusing—but it's true. *Crucifixion is the process of making choices* that destroy selfishness and pride, allowing those traits to be replaced with love and humility.

Anything that feeds our selfishness and our pride has to go. Often that leads to dramatic changes in our jobs, our relationships, and our attitudes. We must always keep in mind that God's objective is not to eliminate fulfillment, just selfishness and pride. When love and humility take over, God has a responsible servant, one with whom He can trust His gift of abundant life.

A consuming passion

The week before Calvary, at the time of Jerusalem's preparations for the Passover feast, Jesus marched into the Temple. Surveying the scene, He made a whip for Himself. He was furious with the profiteers who abused their brethren by turning God's house into a venue for their own selfish gain. Jesus kicked over the tables and began to thrash people with His whip. He drove them out with indignation. Terrified, people ran from His fury.

The disciples must have said to themselves, "Wow! We've never seen Jesus like this before." Then they remembered the Old Testament scripture, "Zeal for Thy house consumes Me."[6] That explained His strong emotions. God's house is not something of casual interest to the Lord; it's His passion, it's at the very center of His heart. Peter said that *we* are the house for which God is so zealous, a house made of living stones. We have a God who is passionately devoted to His people, His church. He wants us to be just as strongly committed.

> Thus says the Lord of hosts: "I am zealous for Zion with great zeal; with great fervor I am zealous for her."[7]

The desire to pursue the purpose of God must exceed every other. Someone who is ready to be part of God's family must be willing not only to make it part of his life; *he must make it the reason for his life.*

Whose dreams?

Not long ago, I was sitting on a park bench talking with someone who had recently made a serious decision to follow God. I was explaining how Jesus came to destroy our selfishness. He wants us to die to our personal ambitions, I said, and live for His. As we were talking, an old acquaintance, a Christian I hadn't seen in years, walked by and stopped to say hello.

I introduced the two, and mentioned my companion's recent decision to follow Jesus. "That's wonderful," the old acquaintance said. Then, as he began commenting, he said something that astounded me.

"Jesus," he declared, "has come to fulfill your dreams."

I stared at him in disbelief. His statement was completely opposite of what I had just been saying.

Did Jesus come to make your fondest desires come true? Is

Jesus' greatest joy to fulfill your dreams? That is not consistent with the message of the Bible. It's the death process that leads to life. Replacing your dreams with God's brings fulfillment.

Have you ever known someone who started out zealous for God, but after ten or twenty years his excitement died? I know a man who was convinced the Lord told him he would make a fortune through a multilevel marketing business. He showed me his dream, which he had pasted up on his refrigerator. He had clipped a picture out of a magazine of a beautiful house with a pool in the backyard. A couple of horses were grazing in a nearby pasture. He told his wife and children, "This is going to be ours."

But they never saw their dream come true. I talked to the man about seven years later. As his success dream had faded, his life had begun to disintegrate. He was separated from his wife; his family, his job, and everything in his life had broken down. He had expected God to preserve his dream, but had learned a hard lesson: God does not necessarily bless whatever dream we claim for ourselves; His blessing is upon *His* dream—His purpose.

People inevitably come into the church with certain ambitions and desires:

"I've been stuck in my hometown all my life. I want to travel and see the world."

"I want to climb to the top of the company."

"I want to record music."

"I want to build a cabin in the wilderness."

"I want to live by the ocean."

"I want to race in the Olympics."

The Lord listens to us, then issues a challenge: "Will you fall in love with what I'm in love with? Will you lay down your dreams that My purpose might be accomplished?"

Our Father is a jealous God. He wants preeminence in our lives. And if we want to enter into His house, there is only one door: the door of death to every ambition, desire, goal, and dream within our hearts that is not connected to the kingdom of

God. Those words correlate with Jesus' statement that unless a man is willing to lose his life, he can't follow Him. You can understand why some people listened to the sayings of Jesus and went away sad. They didn't accept His message and follow Him because it would have cost too much.

Jesus discussed the wisdom of counting the cost. If we launch into a cause without a clear notion of what it will require, we might be inclined to quit when the going gets tough. We need to consider the cost, and then decide if the price is one we are willing to pay.

Barriers

Facing tremendous obstacles is always challenging and often frightening. But if we are serious about wanting to see a church that can have an impact on a disintegrating world, then we must determine to accept the challenge of giving ourselves at whatever cost to God's vision.

The bad news, though, is that several barriers stand between the rather debilitated church of today and the powerful church depicted in the painting we've been discussing. The following chapters deal with specific barriers that believers and local churches must penetrate to become strong and productive. The strategy for overcoming these barriers is simple: crucifixion. We must make choices that place God's desires higher than our own, choices that show our acceptance of God's ways over ours. In the wake of these choices the barriers will fall, allowing us to see God's masterpiece and become part of its grand design.

CHAPTER 12

THE ENVIRONMENT BARRIER

If you spend time with new converts, especially young ones, you will often hear some rash statements about their commitment to God.

"Lord, I'll do anything for You. Just show me Your will. I'll follow You anywhere. Show me where You want me to go."

In the enthusiasm of the moment, when initially struck by the truth of the gospel and overwhelmed by the touch of God, a new Christian finds it easy to make big promises. It's keeping them that is difficult. And the early promises, offered with such innocent sincerity, tend later on to be qualified, revised, and otherwise adjusted.

But what would happen if, when God did reveal His will, He indicated that He wanted you to live someplace where you didn't want to live at all? What if He would have you live someplace where you couldn't take up the career you had dreamed of and had prepared to pursue, or in a place where you just wouldn't have the things you had always wanted to have? Perhaps you would feel that God would be going too far if He actually asked you to set aside your ambitions and preferences, requesting that you invest your years in a local church that happened to be located someplace where the surroundings lacked appeal?

Whether your taste is for the quiet, wide-open spaces of the American West, or for the high-rises and fast pace of Manhattan, most of us have preferences regarding our lifestyles and living situations. If following God means giving up those environmental preferences, are you still willing to be part of His plans?

Over the years I have watched lots of people face this issue. Some have allowed their natural inclinations to guide them to certain areas of the country or into particular living arrangements that fit their desires. That's not to say that God will never lead you in a direction you like. But preferences as to one's environment and one's lifestyle can form a barrier that prevents people from putting their roots down in a local church where God intends for them to live and contribute to the kingdom. Our independent spirits often demand to be left alone when it comes to decisions about where we live.

Goodbye, Idaho

Thom and Ronda came here from Idaho so Thom could get his master's degree at the University of Missouri in Columbia. Thom, an ex-logger who loves the outdoors, dreamed of finishing school, returning to his beloved Pacific Northwest, and getting a job as a forester. Here's Thom sharing his sentiments:

> We really liked Idaho; we had fallen in love with it. It was the most beautiful place I'd been in my whole life. It was open, spacious. You could take a drive and within five minutes be by yourself. There were mountains to climb. Clear streams. Skiing. Fishing. Hunting. Hiking. Camping. Winter sports. Solitude. Then we came to Missouri and found that the woods were full of ticks and chiggers and poison ivy. In summer it was humid and hot. There were few pine trees but plenty of ragweed and pollen.

The mountainless Midwest had little attraction for this outdoorsman accustomed to spectacular scenery. Ronda, who had been raised in the Rockies, yearned to return home. They saw themselves, basically, as biding their time until Thom finished his master's degree. They looked to the day when they would find a place to settle out West, preferably in the high country near some cross-country ski trails and glacier-fed streams.

At the same time, though, they were getting involved in a church where people felt strongly about making the house of God the highest priority in their lives. They were hearing messages about how the Lord wants His church to be "of great magnificence and fame and splendor in the sight of all the nations."[1] They began getting excited about passages in Scripture that identified the church as "the mountain of the [Lord]" that would be "established as chief among the mountains. . . ."[2]

Thom and Ronda began seeing the church as more significant than they had ever known, and a desire grew within them to see the church prosper. Now they were at a difficult crossroads. They could stay in the muggy mid-Missouri plains and remain committed to the cause they had taken up, a cause that had come to mean a great deal to them. Or they could head for the high country they found so enjoyable and hope for the best when it came to finding a church. It was a wrenching decision.

> I [Thom] came to the conclusion that I would be foolish to go back to Idaho. I might have been able to fulfill the natural desire I had for that part of the country, but I would have been turning my back on so much more. Spiritually there was so much God was wanting to do in my heart and with my family, putting us together with the friends we were making here and being involved with what He was doing in the church.
>
> It was very painful realizing that we might not go back to Idaho. But we knew we had to stay, no matter what the sacrifice. It's like selling all you've got for that one pearl. You'd be a fool to walk away from it.

Ronda tells of a time when she was having lunch in a cafe and was reminded of her fondness for the Rocky Mountains:

I looked up and saw a lithograph of the place where Thom and I had spent our honeymoon, Ouray in southern Colorado. Suddenly, all the love I had for the mountains swelled up inside me, and I was just overwhelmed again with a longing for the West. As I was gazing at those mountains a thought came to me, and I felt it was the Lord: "There's a higher calling than 14,000 feet." That set my heart at ease and gave me peace. That was after five years of intense inner struggle.

A dream dissolves

Another couple, Wayne and Donna, also faced the challenge of setting aside their preference for a certain living situation. Wayne is the kind of guy who likes his privacy. Unlike Thom, he was satisfied with the prospect of putting down roots in Missouri. But from his boyhood he has enjoyed the open spaces where nobody's around to get in his way.

The Lord got Wayne's attention during his college days and over a period of years began to change his desires. Wayne, a builder with his own construction business, began to get a vision for the church—for the house that God wanted to build. That dream began to grow within him and his wife, Donna, until it became bigger than their own dreams. Wayne recounts their story.

It was our dream to build a house in the country and to do it ourselves. One thing led to another, and the small, modest house that I had envisioned turned into a beautiful custom home with a unique design.

We built it so it was nestled in the woods, and we went to great lengths to make it blend in with the surroundings. It just kind of evolved until we had a real dream home. But from the start, before we even finished it, we had a really deep sense that it wasn't going to satisfy us.

Wayne and Donna lived in their dream home five years. All during that time, their involvement with our church was expanding. It reached a point where their lives were centered on what was happening in the church: being part of various ministries, building friendships, reaching out to people. Wayne explains what was taking place:

> The whole reason for being in the country was to enjoy it and spend time out there in the serenity. We were isolated. But more and more, our lives were getting wrapped up with the church and the things there that we wanted to be part of. Several nights a week we would drive home from work, eat, and drive back to the church.
>
> We decided that we either had to go one direction or the other: either cut off a lot of activities and relationships and just be out there in the country, or go into town and be a part of things.
>
> The vision of the church was developing, and I think my understanding of things was unfolding. I finally saw the possibilities of what the church could really be. There didn't seem to be anything that made any more sense than just jumping in with both feet even though it went against my natural inclination to think of leaving our place in the country.

Donna said that their time with people in the church had become more enjoyable and more fulfilling than the isolation of the country:

> Neither of us wanted too much involvement when we first came here. We didn't want to get too close to people, and we didn't want them to get too close to us. We wanted our space. That really changed. We didn't want to be isolated any more.

Wayne and Donna now live a stone's throw from the church building. Their house is surrounded by those of other people in the church, so all their neighbors are friends; they could hardly have found a neighborhood with a more people-intensive lifestyle. Neighbors and friends stop by, streams of people walk by on their way to church, teens cluster in their cul-de-sac, and tricycle-riding toddlers overrun their driveway.

They could have had their country life and still have been committed to the church. Nothing's wrong with that; many families in the church live several miles away, some quite a distance, in fact. But Wayne felt God calling him to give up his desire for isolation and move on to something better. Their home has become a hub of ministry and center of hospitality for visiting pastors and guests.

Wayne and Donna made the church their highest priority, higher than that of the secluded country living that was their personal preference. Wayne still loves the quiet, open spaces of the country. That will probably never change. But he has tapped a deeper well of satisfaction than that which could ever come from his natural environment.

I've watched many people follow the principle of laying aside personal preferences. This type of decision is often a prerequisite for God putting a fire in their hearts, a fire that can clear the church of its tarnish and its reputation for weakness.

CHAPTER 13

THE CAREER BARRIER

For most of us, from a young age we began formulating ideas about what we wanted to do when we grew up. As we proceeded through school, perhaps pursuing a college degree, we began to focus on a career direction. There is nothing wrong with that, of course. But what if buying the "pearl of great price"—the kingdom of God—costs you your career dreams? What if it means working for less money or forgoing opportunities for advancement? Or doing something totally different from what you had your heart set on?

Much of the world is trying to move up the career ladder. The process begins in school, as many young people strive for high grades, or popularity, or athletic prowess, all for the sake of the job or position awaiting them down the road. It continues as people graduate and seek positions to match their credentials and desires. Then, after being hired, a person seeks to advance his career however he can: maybe by getting more schooling, working nights and weekends, or relocating to another city. Through it all, people are making choices about their values, their lifestyles, and their priorities.

The problem is that career life is fundamentally self-centered. The company is serving itself by getting the best person available for the job; you're serving yourself by going after the best position you can get. Those who get promoted are those who know how to "play the game." The whole world works that way, because everyone strives to promote his or her own self-interest. But if the church is going to work, it must move in the opposite direction. A person who chooses to devote himself to the purpose of God knows that the pursuit of self-interest no longer has preeminence.

Descending the ladder of success

Most career people like to think of themselves as climbing rung by rung up the ladder that leads to what is commonly considered success: more money, better benefits, more responsibility, higher status. But in the early days of our church, as we were becoming a "family" of believers, people sometimes chose to take a few steps back down that success ladder. Why? So they could remain part of what God was doing. People had a sense that God was calling them together. The sense of commitment was growing deeper, and that was beginning to affect the choices people were making about the future.

One of our church deacons was working as producer and director for a local television station when the church was getting started. His sights were set on New York City or Los Angeles, and he planned to make the move into "big-time" television within a few years. But the church began playing an increasingly important role in his life.

Bob had been coming to our church less than a year when a tremendous career opportunity came his way: the chance to produce Christian television. A Christian broadcasting network executive invited him to go out to the East Coast. The career prospects were attractive: a national show with millions of viewers.

"Come and check it out," the executive told him. "We need people like you."

It seemed like the perfect road to a Christian career with a lot of potential. Yet Bob felt uneasy. He had set himself firmly in the church and was growing spiritually; he was excited about what was happening and about being involved in it. When he asked himself, "Do I want to move away from this?" the answer was no. He never accepted the invitation, and after fifteen years he has yet to regret it. This type of choice became commonplace in the church.

Hamburger helper

Clay was another who decided to plant himself in the church. In 1977 he was teaching school in another town, and was making plans to move to Columbia to pursue a master's degree in business at the University. As he prepared to make the move, he started coming to Columbia on weekends to visit the church. Here he tells his story:

> Since 1974, when I was saved, I'd wanted to be part of a church, but I could never make any connections. I almost became part of one church; then, at the last minute, the job I had fell through and I had to move away. But when I visited this church in Columbia, I felt it was to be my home.
>
> It was then that the Holy Spirit prompted me to begin asking myself some questions. "What do you commit yourself to? Doctrines? Ideas?" That didn't seem appropriate. The next question was: "Do you commit yourself to an organization?" I was too unconventional to sell myself out to some kind of corporate structure. The third question was, "Do you commit yourself to people?" My answer was, "Sure, that's what you do."
>
> Then it was as if the Holy Spirit asked me if I would commit myself to people right here in this town. And I understood that if I answered yes, my plans for business school might be scrapped because my whole purpose for coming would be to make a commitment, a spiritual commitment, to people.

So I just said, "Okay, I'll do it." I thought maybe I would sell shoes or something. I didn't know what it meant. But the Lord didn't stop me from going to business school. The doors were open; the finances were provided, and so on. So God didn't shut that door, but I knew I wasn't to think of myself as being on an educational conveyor belt to be spit out after two years. I wasn't to interview with companies and go off to some big city. I just assumed that as long as the Lord was letting me go to business school, there would be some job for me when I got out. And I believed it would be here in Columbia, because that was all part of His plan.

It was a two-year course of study, and I set days aside to fast and pray to get the job that God wanted for me. When I graduated, I applied every place in town I could think of. But nobody wanted me; I was too educated. Nobody thought I would stay.

I went several months without a job, and I used up what money I had in savings. One day a friend came over and gave me a check just so I could eat. I was bummed out.

Shortly after that I drove by Burger King. I had avoided applying at fast food restaurants, but I asked myself, "Are you too proud?" So many people had turned me down because I had too much education that I thought, "They're not going to hire me there." Just to prove to myself that I wasn't too proud, though, I went in and filled out an application. Before I finished, the manager said, "When do you want to start?"

Clay hired on; he flipped burgers, sacked French fries, and rang up orders. Almost everyone there was in high school; he was thirty-one. He had an MBA and was earning minimum wage.

Several months passed before Clay was able to get off the grill. He still wasn't exactly using his graduate-level training in working as a writer for the state air-pollution control department. But, as a committed member and leader in the church, he was doing what mattered most to him.

Big city money

Others who put their commitment to the church above their careers have chosen to stay in Columbia, even when they had opportunities to earn tens of thousands of dollars more elsewhere. Two physicians in our congregation have both made such choices.

Ellis, a pathologist on the faculty of the local university hospital, met the Lord in 1977. He first came to church when someone invited him to a men's breakfast. He had been part of the church for about seven years when his faculty position appeared to be in jeopardy. Here he explains his response:

It became evident that perhaps I would have to move on. Generally the thing to do would be to look for a job elsewhere because there was no job for me in town. But we decided to stick it out. I told somebody, "Well, I guess I'll stay around to pump gas or something." We weren't sure what we were going to do.

I could go about any place I wanted to because I'm a black guy and a pathologist. I had offers from several different places to make two or three times the salary I'm making here. People were thinking, "You're crazy for staying. Why not go to the big city and make more money and do whatever you want to do?"

It gave me a chance to share what God was doing. I told them that I wasn't staying here because of a job but because of what Jesus was doing in the church, and that I was part of it. I got a chance to share that with almost everybody I work with at the hospital. The chairman of my department knows very clearly that the reason I'm here has nothing to do with my job.

For more than a year I was living one day at a time, trying to figure out, "What am I going to do here? Am I going to start a pathology lab on my own?" I was going to work up a brochure and open my own laboratory consultancy.

I likened it to Abraham not knowing why he was wandering in the wilderness. He just knew that he was looking for a city built by God. It was as if I had something in front of me, but all I could see was the next step. I was confident that God had put us here, and that we were going to stay until He gave us a new direction. This [the church] was our family. It eventually turned out that God provided a way for my job at the hospital to continue.

Tom, a psychiatrist, moved to Columbia to complete his medical training with a three-year psychiatry residency. His perspective on his career changed dramatically in a short time. He explains:

Those first three years were really intense for us. I was very busy. Initially I didn't find the time for the church. I was busy following my own pursuits: looking at how people are made up psychologically, how they think, how they feel. It was toward the end of the residency that God really apprehended me. He actually changed my heart. It was almost like an instantaneous change.

My desire before, the pursuit of my heart, had been for professional excellence—to be the best I could be at what I did. There's a pride in that, an arrogance. God reorganized my heart so that those things just dissipated. What God has done is remove—actually jackhammer— the professional pride that was in me, and that allowed me to lay down my own pursuits.

There's really been a drastic change in my life. Career is not primary. My priority is the church: the people we are sharing our lives with, the people we love.

There are always people trying to recruit you to different positions. I've turned down salaries much higher than what we could make in this town. That's way down on the list as far as I'm concerned.

Tom's wife, Terry, who handles the office duties in his psychiatry clinic, says they regularly receive letters offering a new practice or position. "The salaries range up to $150,000," Terry says, "but we just tear the letters up and throw them away."

Corporate pressure

In some ways the career choices are even harder for those who have already tasted the fruit of success and have watched their careers advance. But usually an organization will, sooner or later, force its workers to choose their priorities.

Dan, a neighbor, held a secure position as an underwriter for one of the nation's leading insurance companies. When his career was going to take him and his family away from town, it put him at a crucial point.

Dan tells the story:

The company I worked for wanted to transfer me to a job in Wichita, Kansas. My superintendent told me the chances were really good that I would be back in Columbia in two years, with another promotion, if I would just take this job in Wichita.

We moved there, but after about eighteen months it became apparent that the company was not going to bring me back in two years. So we began to think and pray seriously about coming back. I wanted my personal relationship with the Lord to grow. I wanted my roots to go deeper.

So one day I walked in and resigned. I told my boss

I wanted to move back to Columbia, that I was committed to my church and wanted to be a part of establishing it. I told him that it was best for my own personal growth and for my family's. It was a decision I needed to make because the Lord was a priority in my life.

He said, "Please don't resign. Think about it." I told him my decision was final.

"Do you understand what you're doing to your career?" people said. "You're only thirty-two years old, and there's a lot of opportunity ahead of you."

Dan didn't reconsider. He had determined that his job and the financial rewards it promised were not as important as the local church he believed God had made him a part of.

Dan's quitting date was approaching when his boss telephoned to offer him his old job in Columbia, although it meant a demotion in position and salary. Dan accepted:

After getting back, I was subjected to conversations and meetings at work about my future and how I had just ruined a good career. I just made up my mind that not only was I committed to seeing the church established, but that I was going to give my job every effort I could as well.

Even though I had some down times, I can say that my attitude was good because of what the Lord was doing in my life. Looking back, I'm glad I did it. There's no question in my mind that it was the right decision for my own spiritual well-being as well as for my family's.

A different kind of church

As Christians, we need to be loyal and dedicated employees, of course. But our first loyalty and first love must be for God's kingdom. That goes against the direction in which the world is moving, and so causes friction. If you adopt this mentality, people will accuse you of being too radical. But the Bible is a radical book. And the body of Christ needs churches that give people the opportunity to fully live out the radical message of the gospel. Believers need to be challenged to throw everything they've got into fulfilling the purpose of God by committing themselves to a local church.

We're promoting the kind of church that says, "The local church can work. Jesus said He would build His church, and we're going to devote ourselves to making that a reality in our midst. Let's serve God with everything we've got." We want churches composed of people willing to climb off the career ladder, if the choice comes down to that, because they want to build something much, much bigger than a career.

Some of the men and women in our church who have given up employment opportunities in other cities have found even better jobs here, great jobs. Many of these people, though, at the time they made their decision, had no guarantee of any work at all.

Is it safe?

This kind of talk will stir up all kinds of fears. In the minds of many, to devote oneself to a local church is a risky proposition. How can they be sure the church will stay together? What if it falls apart, like so many other churches have?

That is a legitimate question. It's a fact that relationships can break down, that seemingly faithful people can reneg on previous promises. Congregations can disband. People can stray from God. A church can be built on faulty foundations, and things can just generally go to pieces. It happens. But that does not change the fact that God is going to build His church; He has promised that He will. The price remains high, though. Some believers will offer themselves to be used fully for God's purposes, and others will not, deterred by the cost.

Giving a career top priority in your life sounds right because everyone promotes that idea. But what about the people who get fired, and those who can't find a job in their field? What about the employees laid off when a company is sold, goes bankrupt, or relocates? The point is this: circumstances can easily derail someone's career. You can bet your future on a career, but it's still a gamble.

A costly career

Pete was a man who devoted himself totally to his career with a multinational retailing firm. Part of the price he paid for advancement was uprooting his family every two or three years as the company promoted him to higher positions.

He was a wealthy man with a six-figure annual income when he walked into work one day and was fired. After twenty-seven years of corporate loyalty, he became a casualty of the company's efforts to streamline its management structure. He was replaced by someone who was paid less than half his salary.

His son, who is in our church, also works for a large corporation. But he has placed his commitment to the church above his career advancement. He turned down his company's offer to put him on the "fast track" to upper management because they required "total mobility." His decision has cost him some salary increases and has slowed his rise to management positions; nonetheless, he makes a living that provides his family a nice home and a comfortable lifestyle. Losing his job would be a blow, but it wouldn't be the tragedy that struck his father.

Pete's life began to self-destruct, a process exacerbated by his alcoholism, and within three years he declared bankruptcy. The crisis snowballed, and eventually he was forced to leave his wife and seek a haven in the home of his son—and his son's church. At the peak of his professional life, in his mid-50s, he recognized that his choices had led to disaster. During his stay here, where he got help sorting out his life and coping with his devastation, he commended his son's decisions to put his church rather than his career first.

Against the tide

People like those mentioned in this chapter made courageous decisions, swimming against the strong current in society that says career comes first. Their choices make it clear that the church isn't something they just tacked onto their lives *after* everything else was in place.

The untold portions of the testimonies just recounted would reveal how often the act of sacrifice comes full circle. Several of the people whose stories you have just read are enjoying careers and financial rewards above and beyond what they originally laid down in order to follow God.

These people believe that building the church is God's top priority, and they have made it theirs as well. They aren't asking God to help them realize their personal ambitions. They have adjusted their own ambitions to align them with God's desire for a magnificent church. In doing so they have found that as they follow God, He will lead them through seasons of sacrifice as well as abundance. God's blessing, though, is constantly present for those who choose His way above any other.

CHAPTER 14

THE FAMILY
BARRIER

If anyone comes to me and does not hate his father and mother,
his wife and children, his brothers and sisters—yes, even his own
life—he cannot be my disciple. — Luke 14:26

If someone makes it his life's passion to see the church of God restored in his own generation, inevitably there will be those in his natural family who will not understand.

They won't understand the sacrifices he makes, for instance in altering his career goals, if it comes to that. They won't understand why he gives so generously of his hard-earned income, why he doesn't have more leisure time, why he seems to be "making life harder than it has to be." These questions and the pressures they bring are part of the price we must pay if we are committed to working for a church that matches the picture of a place set in "praise, fame, and honor high above all the nations."[1] Often, connections with our families can become another barrier between us and our participation in God's design.

Family pressure

At times I have found it difficult to explain to my own family—
my parents and relatives—what I am doing with my life. This
was especially so during my first years as a believer.

I come from a family of hard-working people. My father, a
second-generation Italian-American, opened a television repair
business in his native Brooklyn, N.Y., not long after televisions
were introduced. During my years growing up, his skill in
business became evident. He branched out into other business
ventures, eventually developing a multimillion dollar enterprise.
He always wanted me to join him in the business. There was an
office in New York waiting for me whenever I wanted it.

While in Bible college, and for the first few years after
graduation, my wife and I had some rough times financially. I
was an assistant pastor, with a salary that covered the rent, the
light bill, groceries, and little more. My wife, Dawn, got sick
during her pregnancy. We didn't have the money for a private
doctor, so our first baby was born through a welfare clinic
program.

When hard times hit, my father could have offered to help us
financially, but he didn't. "You made your choice," he said.
"You've got to live with it." My father loved my family and me
dearly, but he purposely decided to wait and see whether or not
I would stick to what I was doing, even under pressure. He made
the right choice.

"If you change your mind," he would tell me, "you can come
help me run the business." He was not asking me to renounce
my faith or do anything immoral or illegal. "You can still be a
Christian and work for me," he said. "Come on, I need your
help."

During this time I always felt torn. I felt constrained by God
to do what I was doing in the church, but I couldn't really explain
that to my parents. I believed that God had given me a vision for
the church, and I had to devote myself to it. That was how it had
to be, even if it meant creating a family division that I didn't want.

I love my family; I express that to them, and our relationships have always been close. That closeness, however, did not prevent a lengthy period of tension among us. I went through a long period—years, in fact—during which my family was quite upset with me. My parents were Catholic and had raised their children in that church. So they had a difficult time when their son, living in Berkeley, California, suddenly announced that he had "gotten saved." They were worried sick that I had been taken in by some strange cult. They pleaded with me to see a priest or a psychiatrist; my father even boarded a plane and flew out to investigate. He gained some assurance that I hadn't gone completely off the deep end, but it was not until years later that he began understanding more about my life and my cause and even experienced his own second birth.

Those early years brought some rough moments. In my outspoken family, strong wills, strong emotions, and strong opinions come as standard equipment. Normal dinner conversation would often heat up into an argument over the subject of my involvement in the church. Also, no one in my family had ever moved away from New York, and they felt slighted because from their perspective I had abandoned them.

Maternal understanding

My mother, one of the most outspoken people in the family, flew more than 1,000 miles to attend my Bible college graduation and watch me pass this milestone into ministry. She didn't like what she saw. She told me I had wasted four years of my life.

We want to preserve harmony in families. We don't want to stir up conflict. But when God plants His vision inside you, it is going to run contrary to your natural desires, thoughts, and inclinations. All the natural things within us that hold us back from pursuing that vision have to die; and as you make those choices, you will find that your decisions won't always be popular with your family. Jesus said that such things would happen.

Do you think I came to bring peace on earth? No, I tell

you, but division. From now on there will be five in one
family divided against each other, three against two
and two against three.[2]

Parents especially are often wary of radical commitments.
I've had some parents of college-age kids in my congregation
become very upset with me, and have found myself in
conversations like this:
"What's going on?" the parents might ask. "I sent my son off
to college and all of a sudden he doesn't want to follow his
career. He wants to stay so he can keep going to this church.
Now he's a college graduate, and he has taken a menial job." It's
difficult to explain to a parent that God gave his child a vision
for the church, one that will cause him to lay aside opportunities
for personal gain. Very rarely is that explanation comforting. But
as time passes a different perspective often emerges.

Full circle

We need to remember that God wants our families to see the life
He offers us, not just to be upset over our decisions to follow
Him. Through the years I have watched a dramatic transformation
in my own family. Their skepticism has turned to loyalty and
enthusiasm for what I am doing.

My father passed away recently, leaving a vacuum in my
family that is impossible to fill. I am deeply grateful to God for
revealing Himself to my father several years ago, and am
comforted by knowing I will be with him again. Memories of the
early years of tension disappear in the face of the tangible
support my father later provided, including generous gifts that
have blessed our whole church.

With his passing, my mother needs me more than before, and
I have made several trips to New York to help put my father's
business affairs in order. While I was there the thought struck me
that I had done little to lighten my father's workload over the

years, and, now that he's gone, I am constrained by my responsibilities in our church. My mother must have been reading my thoughts, because she sat down next to me and put my mind at ease.

"Joseph," she told me, "whatever you do, don't leave the church. Your father and I wouldn't want you to do that."

Sympathetic grandparents

Our church was founded by a group of people who made some radical commitments: they gave up dreams, often making considerable sacrifice, because the church was the most significant thing in their lives. Many of them ran into conflict with their parents, who, like all parents, wanted their children to be happy and to succeed in life, and who saw the church as something that got in the way.

But we have watched an interesting development take place. These "idealistic" youths have turned into adults and have become parents themselves, and their parents have watched the sons and daughters and grandchildren grow up. They have come to visit; they have seen the lifestyle their offspring have adopted and the friendships they have made, and they like what they see.

"You know," they'll say, "my son ended up with a decent job. He has a nice house and a wonderful family. And that church he's in, with all those caring people—that's a great place for my grandkids to grow up. But more than that, my son has got some of the best friends you can imagine; people have really cared about him through the years. I've never had friendships like the ones my son has."

Parents come and wish they had what their children have. They feel the power of the church, and they see that God is in it. They see joyful people sharing their lives with one another. Their sons and daughters are not just trying to scratch out an existence on their own; they have linked themselves with the family of God, and their life together is a beautiful testimony of God's love and grace.

My cousin, a vice president for a global advertising firm, spends most of his time flying all over the world to conduct business for his company. He's a man who can afford a lifestyle that's beyond the reach of most people. But when he comes to visit our church, he sees something he doesn't have, something he could never buy: he sees genuine affection, lasting friendship, people relating on a heart-to-heart level rather than with the skin-deep superficiality that prevails in his world; and he's envious. He thinks deeply about life and is not impressed with the accumulation of things or a higher position in a company. He has achieved the American dream, but he knows he still doesn't have what he wants. He could set his sights on a chalet in the Swiss Alps or a condominium overlooking the white sands of Maui; but the last time he visited, he started talking about coming to be part of a church in central Missouri, of all places.

Mothers and fathers, brothers and sisters

We have seen proof of God's promise that anyone who loses the benefits of natural family life for the sake of the gospel will become part of an even larger family within the church. Pam, a black woman who has been part of our church for more than ten years, has experienced this principle in her life.

> I grew up in an all-black world in a housing project in Kansas City. There was an unwritten code: "You do not socialize with or befriend 'them'"—white people. That unwritten code remained in my heart. In college I soaked in the philosophies of Malcolm X. I idolized Angela Davis. Hearing her speak at the university was like a dream come true. In a philosophical way, I was in the "black power" movement.
> So when I came to church here I was in a dilemma. I had been saved, and loved God, but there were all these people—and they weren't black. They were trying to crowd into my life, wanting to talk to me and

befriend me, but I didn't want people close to me. For the first time I saw that I really was "standoffish."

In my family, I grew up as a very quiet, introverted child. I never felt close or experienced what I would consider intimacy with a lot of people in my family. I didn't have any tools with which to build relationships because I didn't know how. It's not something I grew up with.

In the church, I'm learning these things first-hand: how you open up your heart with a mother and receive counsel, nurturing, instruction, and love. How you can be open with your father and have a heart-to-heart talk, and have him give direction for your life. Because of my own fears and inhibitions, mostly, I didn't open up with my own father. So, it's been here in the church that people like Elias [a leader in the church] have been a father to me. Elias sat me down, talked to me and corrected me, and he has loved us. Diane, his wife, has been like a mother to me, and so has Lou [another spiritually mature woman]. My kids call her Nana. She talks to me about things that I never talked to my mother about. And sisters—I can't even count how many sisters I have. These are relationships that I have never experienced anywhere except in the church.

People like Pam are experiencing the benefits Jesus promised to those who abandon all their natural securities, break their cultural ties, and risk becoming vulnerable to people.

No one who has left home or brothers or sisters or mother or father or children or fields for me and the gospel will fail to receive a hundred times as much in this present age.[3]

Jesus said that the rewards of seeking first the kingdom aren't just waiting for you in heaven. When you make God's family a priority in your life, you reap the benefits of being a family member—in this life, in your local church.

CHAPTER 15

THE
POSSESSIONS
BARRIER

Our church met for three years in a shopping center. On warm nights we would keep the front doors propped open for ventilation. During worship, curious shoppers from the supermarket next door would sometimes wander in, grocery bags in hand, to see what the music was all about.

Those were casual days, and with only a moderate rent payment and two salaries to pay, our overhead was easy to manage. But as the church grew our facility became less and less suitable. The decision to buy property and construct a building intensified our practical responsibilities.

The fires of sacrifice

The first problem, as usual, was money. That age-old obstacle has thrown a big wrench into the greatest of plans. Wouldn't it be nice, we thought, for God to send a wealthy land baron who would be converted, donate his land, and pay for a building. That is no doubt the prayer of every pastor whose church faces the possessions barrier. No pain. No pressure. We could have just waltzed into our promised land with our bank accounts intact, and our free time undiminished.

But for any church to become strong, the people must pass through the fires of sacrifice. To buy the picture God had painted before our minds' eyes, we had to empty our wallets, then our bank accounts. We emptied our houses of some cherished possessions. And, as if that wasn't enough in the way of sacrifice, we then had the privilege of working together—much of it strenuous manual labor—for months on end to construct the physical facilities that would accommodate the type of church we were believing God would build.

Our money

In the absence of a present-day J.D. Rockefeller, we resorted to the only fund-raising option available to us: selling bonds. That was the only option simply because none of the banks would lend us money, and even if everyone in the church gave everything they had, the total certainly would not have reached the $150,000 needed for the thirty-five acres we wanted.

Two representatives from a bond company came to Columbia to make the arrangements. We got the impression they were accustomed to more traditional, well-endowed congregations. They were not prepared for what they encountered.

When they walked in, they discovered that our church met in a storefront: we had been dubbed "the church in the marketplace." My office was at the front of what once had been a furniture showroom. Two of its walls were large display windows.The one in front was graced by a bullet hole. Before we put up curtains the window shoppers would sometimes gaze into my office, curious about why I was sitting at a desk in a showroom window. With all my pastoral dignity, I would wave at them.

Inside, the place wasn't exactly the Sistine Chapel. We used plastic chairs instead of padded pews. Instead of chandeliers on the ceiling we had exposed water pipes. The one toilet seemed to back up whenever you needed it most. The back wall had an interesting feature, too: the musicians had glued it, top to bottom, with gray egg cartons. (This was supposed to do something for the acoustics.) The fire marshall eventually made us tear the cartons down, but the big gobs of glue would not budge. The wall looked like it had come down with a bad case of chicken pox.

Then there was the congregation, about 150 of us in those days. Many were penniless college students; the rest were not far enough out of college to have much money. Some rode to church on bicycles and hardly anyone owned a house. These were the people who were supposed to buy $150,000 in bonds. The more the two bond company representatives saw, the more distressed they became.

I knew they were not overly optimistic about our success when they flipped a coin to determine their assignments. The winner got to help launch another bond drive for a more prosperous church in Kansas City. The one who lost the toss, a man named Bill, got to stay and help us.

Bill presented us with the idea of going door-to-door to some of the businesses in town, trying to persuade them to buy bonds to help support this new church in the community. He figured it would take several weeks of door-knocking to come up with $150,000.

We started the drive to sell bonds at our Sunday service. Against Bill's better judgment, we did not put out any slick brochures. No big thermometers were tacked on the wall to measure progress. We didn't even ask for a show of hands to see who would participate. A high-pressure pitch just was not our style; we simply explained to the church the financial need and the practical strategy being used to meet it.

The next day, people from the church went to the bank and began taking out personal loans. Within four days the congregation and a few others had bought up $150,000 in bonds. Bill could hardly believe it. His comment to the church was unforgetable. "Either you guys are smack dab in the middle of God's will," he said, "or else you're the luckiest bunch of suckers I've ever seen."

How did it happen? People had a vision for building God's church, and they understood that it was not going to come cheaply. Like King David, they could say, "the house to be built for the Lord should be of great magnificence and fame and splendor. . . . Therefore I will make extensive preparations for it."[1] Looking around, all you could see were young idealists in a vacant furniture store with a broken toilet and egg-carton walls. But in the minds of everyone taking part was this dream of the magnificent house God was building. That is what stirred people to give.

Our time

Once we had purchased the thirty-five-acre site, we started developing the plans for a subdivision along with the church. Our undeveloped land needed water lines, sewers, streets, and so on, before we could subdivide or construct a building. The process of obtaining those necessities was not easy, and the price was not cheap. In fact, when we were quoted the total cost my heart sank. I told the engineer we had hired to plan our subdivision that none of the bids were acceptable. After the bidders left the room he asked me what I was going to do. "We'll do it ourselves," I said, to which he replied, "You can't." We did.

God seems to enjoy placing His people in challenging and suspenseful situations. We had a few skilled volunteers and a man with a construction business and a backhoe, but everyone worked, skilled or not. We paid a small full-time crew, but the bulk of the job was done by dozens of volunteers who literally got down into the trenches. They scrambled in and out of ditches, hauled pipe, swung picks, and pitched dirt. It was dirty, difficult work. Shoveling the Missouri clay is like digging in cement: when it rains, the clay turns into a heavy sludge that sticks in great globs to the shovel. But the men kept moving dirt and laying pipe until the job was done. It took months of spare evenings and Saturdays.

When the subdivision was well underway we started building the church, a steel structure that was erected in four phases.

Construction work has been an ongoing process for us. One section of the building would be completed, then a year or two or three would pass, and the construction work would begin again on another phase. Now, with the sanctuary, two wings of classrooms, a full-length gym with locker rooms and racquetball courts, a commercial-size kitchen, a publishing operation, and more than a dozen offices, the building stretches longer than a football field.

The step of moving out of the storefront required years of hard work and sacrificial giving. But the process of building together has been as beneficial as the final product.

Our possessions

There are landmarks in all of our lives that we can point to as clear signs of life-changing events. Our church passed such a landmark, one that exists as a memorial for us of an experience that positively and dramatically affected our relationships with God and each other.

The Bible tells of three young Hebrews who were taken captive in the Babylonian siege of Jerusalem and were in the service of the king of Babylon.[2] During this time the king erected a huge golden image and commanded that everyone bow down and pay homage to the shrine at an appointed time.

The three Hebrew men refused to bow, and made it clear to the king that they would never pay homage to him. Their insubordination was to be punished by death in the fiery furnace. The men had placed their lives on the line out of faithfulness to God.

The enraged king had commanded that the furnace be made seven times hotter than usual. In the normal course of events you wouldn't expect the men to last very long; they would endure agony for a short while and then die. But that is not what happened. When the king looked inside the furnace, he was astonished at what he saw.

"Did we not cast three men into the furnace?" he asked. His servants answered yes.

"Look!" the king exclaimed. "There are four men walking in the furnace, and the fourth is like the Son of God."

This story struck a chord in my heart. Why doesn't the Bible tell us what went on during the time they spent in the furnace? What did those three young men experience? I felt compelled to know the answers. The response that came to me seemed frightening, "You need to get in the furnace to find out."

"Lord, how can I do that?"

"Through sacrifice," came the reply. "There is a level of fellowship with Me that can only come through sacrifice."

I shared the story with our church, and this led us to a season of sacrifice, a time we came to know as "furnace fellowship." This understanding and acceptance of a difficult spiritual principle turned a fund-raising project into a profound time of spiritual growth that continues to pay dividends in our relationships with God and each other.

This furnace fellowship message came just before an auction we had planned in order to take the fund-raising effort a step further. Everyone who was willing would donate items, and the proceeds would go to the building project. Paul, a public school teacher, and Sandy, a college student in dietetics, participated in this season of sacrifice. Here Paul tells what happened.

> I had been working four years in teaching, and my salary was pretty low. I had been able to tithe regularly, but I didn't have much money saved that I could sacrifice.
>
> Sandy and I had just gotten engaged, and I wanted to see her participate. I wasn't really looking for an amount of money so much as I wanted to see that she was really behind what was going on. I was thinking that her only possession, the only thing that meant a whole lot to her, was her engagement ring.

At one service we were asked to indicate on a piece of paper what we were going to sacrifice. Sandy walked up with me to put our slips of paper in the basket. I put a check in, and she put in a piece of paper. Afterward, I said, "What did you give?"

I could tell she was afraid to tell me. She was shaking. She said she really wanted to participate but since she was supported entirely by her parents and had no money of her own, the only thing of value she could give was her engagement ring. She thought I was going to be mad, because I had spent a lot of money on that ring. I smiled and told her that it really blessed me because that's what I was hoping she would give.

When a girl gets engaged, she's aware of everyone noticing her ring. Her sorority sisters immediately noticed it was gone. They, along with many others, were asking, "Where is your ring?" Suddenly the reality of the sacrifice confronted her. It was easier to participate in the sacrifice with the support of church members, but now she had to deal with the disapproval of friends who couldn't understand how someone could give away her engagement ring. That was hard.

But after she started talking about it her confidence grew, and it opened up a lot of avenues for talking about the depth of her relationship with God and the value of His church.

Without telling Sandy, I made arrangements to have someone come to the auction and bid on her ring for me. I kept all that a secret for several months, then gave the ring to her so she could wear it on our wedding day.

Frank and Traci, a college-age couple who had joined the church as the building project was getting underway, took part in the sacrificial giving. First they gave the $600 they had in their savings account. Then they searched for a way to participate in the auction:

> The only thing we had left of any value was a stereo that Traci's parents had purchased for her at college. We didn't know what it was worth, probably several hundred dollars. We put it in the auction and were glad for the chance to do it. But we dreaded immensely the thought of Traci's parents ever finding out that we'd given away the stereo.
>
> Weeks after the auction we were visiting her parents for the weekend. Late one afternoon our conversation drifted to the topic of home furnishings. We'd moved into our first apartment a few months earlier and Traci and her mom were discussing ways to best arrange our things. Her mom asked how we planned to use the stereo.
>
> We fought off the urge to faint. Then Traci said, "We gave it at the sacrifice auction at church."
>
> They were upset. They were concerned because we were limping along financially anyway. I don't know if they understood that we were giving a tithe [ten percent of one's income] to the church, but they knew that we were giving. They felt that, because of our circumstances, we just couldn't afford that. Now we had given away the stereo.
>
> They made the point that they had given it as a gift, and we replied that we had not intended to hurt them. We really appreciated the stereo. But, we said, it was ours, and we had just chosen of our own volition to give it away. And really, we said, compared to a lot of things people gave, it was insignificant.
>
> Actually, down the road, it has turned out well. I think it indicated to Traci's parents how serious we were. It caused them to take a closer look at the church,

but not in an adversarial way. I think they were quietly intrigued.

Paul and Sandy and Frank and Traci are typical of the people in the church, who have at times made large sacrifices—their time, their money, their possessions—to see the church advance.

Painful sacrifice

As the pastor, I was having a difficult time watching people put things on the auction block, all these possessions that meant so much to them: family heirlooms, wedding rings, treasured keepsakes. It was gripping. I felt like stepping in and saying, "No, don't give that. It's too big a sacrifice." At times I was moved to tears. But it was Jesus who said that where our treasure is, there our hearts will be also. These people, in giving up things that were to them treasures, like a $600 savings account, a nice stereo, or an engagement ring, were making a profound statement about what they treasured most.

I don't want to give the impression that nobody in our church has any personal possessions of value because they've all been given to the church. That's not the case; we have many people who own lovely homes and drive nice new cars, and there's nothing wrong with that. This account is not intended to try to give an impression of any superior spirituality on our part, nor to give anyone a fund raising idea. We have been a church for over a decade and have had only one of these auctions.

The depth of love in any relationship will be measured at times by what it costs us. Our relationship with God is no exception. It will cost us even in the area of possessions. Remember, God's goal is not to take your treasure; it is to capture your heart. That is a principle every group of believers must practice if they want a healthy church.

Once the sacrifices are made, the Lord in many instances gives back in superabundance. Sometimes the "return" comes in the way of a deeper faith or a greater dependence on God; sometimes it can be measured in dollars and cents. In all cases, the giver always receives the benefits of advancing the cause of God in His own generation.

I do not believe that God will make us rich through some tidy prosperity principle, like "Give Me a dollar, and I'll give you two." God has not promised to make us all wealthy, although He has repeatedly promised to richly bless His nation, with blessings of His choosing, how and when He sees fit. My experience tells me, though, that rich blessing does not come without sacrifice—heavy sacrifice.

Treasuring what God treasures

Some outside the church see the degree of sacrifice involved and think that somehow church members must have been manipulated or mesmerized. They don't see how, without controlling their lives, you can get a group of people to pitch in together with such devotion. But pressure tactics, mind games, and authoritarianism have no place in the church; people must have complete freedom to make their own choices. Coercion is a tool of the flesh, which produces death; the law of the Spirit is liberty, which produces life.

The only way a local church will thrive is if people are motivated from *within*, by a desire to love God and pour out their time, their money, their possessions for Him. The most powerful motivator is a loving relationship. When God pours His Spirit upon us, it causes us to love the things He loves and treasure the things He treasures. This motivation causes people to give even beyond what they thought they were capable of giving.

The possessions barrier could have easily squelched God's

purpose for this local church. Penetrating it took everything we had. But once again, the congregation did not shy away from the challenge of sacrificial giving. They felt that the cause to which they were committed was worth the investment.

CHAPTER 16

THE
MINISTRY
BARRIER

So far, the barriers we have discussed are relatively easy to identify. The Bible is straightforward in its instructions about handling your possessions, for example. But when we step beyond actions and begin dealing with attitudes, some of the barriers are a little trickier to spot.

A misdirected attitude toward ministry is one of the more serious barriers hindering the church today. Far too many Christians equate ministry with importance, excitement, and attention rather than with the meniality, monotony, and obscurity of basic servanthood. They think a low-status, behind-the-scenes ministry is demeaning. They want to work on their favorite Christian activities, and they would prefer a job with a title, and some limelight.

Family chores

Imagine how that kind of attitude would work in a family. Dad says, "Well, we've got chores to do. Let's get to work."

Johnny says, "I'll water the grass because I want to play in the sprinkler." Susie says, "I'll bake cookies." And Pete volunteers to wash the car because he's going to use it that evening.

The tasks the children chose for themselves may not be the tasks that most need to be done. It could be that the garage needs sweeping, the dishes need washing, and the baby's diaper needs changing. Given their preference, the kids will rarely choose to do these "dirtier" jobs, from which they get no direct benefit. What kind of a household would that family have if that attitude were allowed to prevail?

The 'My Ministry Syndrome'

Of course, as Christians, we quickly learn the language of ministry. Rather than saying, "I want to do what *I* want to do," you say something like, "I want to allow God to use the gifts and abilities He's given me." In the most serious cases, the individual insists that he is the only one who can discern what gifts God has given him and how they should be employed in the church. We have seen this in dozens of people who have passed through our church. And I do mean "passed through," because they tend not to stay long.

After attending one Sunday service here, a fellow made an appointment with one of the church leaders. He wanted to let us know he was available for "ministry." He wanted to play in the orchestra; he wanted to help produce our publications; he wanted to get involved teaching children. He was gung ho, eager to lead a ministry.

"Your enthusiasm is really great," the leader told him. "But why don't you put your desire for ministry on the shelf for the time being? I suggest you take our foundations class and start getting to know people." That wasn't what he wanted to hear. He wanted a ministry, and he didn't want to wait. When it didn't materialize within six months, he was gone.

The traveling musician

Another man who had been coming to church a short time visited one of the home group meetings. He was excited about the Lord and enthusiastic about all that happened, particularly the worship. He loved to sing, and he especially loved to play the guitar. He told the home group leader how much he loved music and how he had been involved in Christian music ministry before. He wanted to bring his guitar next time and help lead worship. Elsewhere, perhaps, his offer would have been accepted without hesitation. But we have found it better to apply the brakes rather than the accelerator when an unknown, untested believer wants to step into the ministry of his own choosing.

Musicians and singers in particular are involved in a high-profile ministry; they're up on the platform leading the congregation in worship. Their attitudes about what they are doing are critical, and the church gains nothing from someone who wants mostly to show off his abilities. That attitude draws attention away from the Lord and onto the performer—exactly the opposite of what should happen in worship. So no matter how much talent someone might have, nobody can just walk into our church one day and become a church musician the next. People normally are asked to wait for a time before being considered for ministry.

The home group leader in the situation described above did not go into any long explanations about his decision. He politely told the guitar player something like, "I appreciate the offer, but we prefer not to do that at present." Nobody in the church ever saw that man again. He was offended at not getting to play.

People afflicted with this mentality, which I've dubbed the "My Ministry Syndrome," go looking for a church or ministry where their talents are in demand. But their involvement hinges on whether or not they can express their "gifting in God." They inevitably become unhappy if they feel that their abilities are not recognized or fully appreciated. Also, if anything appears to put their ministry in jeopardy—say, for example, they have to take a back seat to someone more talented who comes along—then they're going to be upset. And before long, they're going to leave.

An abundance of teaching has steeped believers in the notion that every one has to have his or her own ministry. Some believers feel almost as if it's their scriptural right to fill out their own ministry ticket. That attitude translates into this selfish-sounding declaration: "I want a position. God has given me a gift, and I want to use it."

Believers like this can end up wandering from group to group, from church to church, looking for a ministry in which their unique talents and gifts can be put to use. God does call people to serve in various capacities, but too often people who feel "called to ministry" embark on a relentless search for an assignment from God. Then, if such a person thinks the tasks he is asked to perform are not part of his "ministry," he feels that the assignment did not come from God and is therefore not necessarily valid.

I once heard about a conversation between an older Christian, whom we'll call Jane, and a friend of hers whom we'll call Susan. Susan was upset with the people in her church; she felt they were not taking advantage of her potential for ministry. I didn't hear about all the specifics. Maybe she had a knack for working with kids and wanted to start a puppet ministry. Or maybe she was a theater buff and wanted to organize a dramatic production. Whatever her ability was, she felt it was going to waste.

"Did you tell the pastor?" Jane asked. Susan replied that she had done so and that the pastor had said he didn't feel the time was right for launching the ministry Susan was interested in.

"What should I do?" she asked her friend.

"If you have a calling in ministry," Jane advised, "you should go find a church where you can use your ministry."

Why did Jane counsel her friend to leave her church? Not because Susan didn't have an important part to play there, but because she did not get the part she wanted. Surely there was opportunity to serve. Jane was telling Susan, though, that she needed to find a church where she could serve on her own terms.

Suppose Susan were to go to another church and find a ministry where she could "fulfill her calling." What would she do if, after a while, she wasn't getting the satisfaction she had hoped to receive from that ministry? Wouldn't it be time for her to move on again? In this way of thinking, a Christian's first loyalty is to his calling rather than to his church. The first priority becomes to make sure your talents and gifts are fully used; that moves your commitment to your brethren far down the priority list. While outwardly the focus is on serving others, inwardly the motivation is fundamentally selfish.

Self-serving ministry

People operating in the My Ministry mode strive to get, build, and preserve their own ministries. They do this for a variety of reasons. Some people want to feel that their unique talents are needed, wanted, valued. If they sense that this is so, they feel good about themselves. Either consciously or unconsciously, it meets a need to feel significant and secure.

Christians say, of course, that they find their significance and their security in the Lord. But all too often, they really get their sense of significance from what *they do* for the Lord. People can feel important by saying, "I'm in the music ministry," or "I'm a youth leader," or "I take care of the church benevolence projects." Ministry becomes just another way of gratifying one's own needs. Rather than approaching it as self-sacrifice, people can seek ministry as a means of self-fulfillment. Hence, their service to the Lord has strings attached. They give only as long as they receive satisfaction in return.

In some instances, the My Ministry Syndrome is fueled by the desire for personal success; it's simply selfish ambition couched in spiritual jargon. People like this are keenly interested in ministry as long as it's theirs.

Motivations such as these produce big problems. They poison many of the work places of the world, and their effect is even worse in the church. When everyone is "looking out for number one," relationships break down. Egos get bruised. Resentments build. People get jealous and jockey for position. The whole system provokes pride rather than humility, competition rather than cooperation, envy rather than a desire to see others succeed. Self-centered ministry doesn't build the church, it destroys it.

The My Ministry menace often goes unrecognized because it is cloaked in spiritual garb. But this cancer, spreading like a plague across the landscape of Christianity, has built a strong barrier that prevents the church from experiencing the life God has in mind.

'What I'm part of . . .'

The theological root of the My Ministry Syndrome is a rejection of the church as the nation of God. Lacking a corporate vision, it's every man for himself. The vision for a nation is replaced with a vision for position. We've discovered in our church that Me-centered ministry perspectives begin to fade as people start taking their eyes off themselves and get a broader view of what God wants to accomplish. That happens as people begin getting a vision to build a strong church, one in which they set aside their personal longings in order to pursue God's desire for a glorious church. When people are motivated by this vision, any one person's particular role in ministry isn't as important as the corporate success of the church. People adopt the attitude, *"What I'm part of is more important than the part I play."*

I enjoy preaching, but if my deepest satisfaction is found in seeing God's house prosper, not in giving sermons, then I won't be devastated if someday I lose the opportunity to preach. Whether the task is preaching the message, setting up chairs, scrubbing pots and pans, or cleaning the restrooms, the goal is always the same: to build the church, to express the heart of God.

Function and desire

To penetrate the My Ministry barrier, believers who want to build the church need to understand the difference between two key words: *function* and *desire.*

Function refers to your particular job or role. You might call this your ministerial calling, the part you play. Different members of the body of Christ have different functions: we have mothers, fathers, pastors, cooks, custodians, deacons, secretaries, businessmen, and so on.

Desire has to do with our motivation. Desire is directed toward the final result, what you're part of. Someone with desire wants to reach the goal however he can; how he gets there is of less concern than actually fulfilling his desire. The Bible more often directs our attention toward the desires God wants us to have than toward the functions we will perform on our way to the goal. Godly actions spring from godly desires. Spiritual function lasts only a short time, but spiritual desire will last for eternity.

In Psalms, we do not find David praying about his function: "Make me a king, Lord. I'll do a better job than Saul, Lord. Give me the throne for Your glory, Lord." No, it's David's *desire* that comes through, his desire for God.

> My soul yearns, even faints for the courts of the Lord;
> my heart and my flesh cry out for the living God.[1]

> As the deer pants for streams of water, so my soul pants
> for you, O God.[2]

David had an intense longing for God, and that desire consumed his heart and his mind. He didn't fret about his function. He wasn't seeking after Saul's throne. "I would rather be a doorkeeper in the house of my God," he said in Psalm 84:10, "than dwell in the tents of the wicked." He became king, but that was not the delight of his heart. His joy came from being part of the house of God.

The Jonathan mentality

Jonathan, King Saul's son, was someone else who showed little concern for his position. All his life, Jonathan was being groomed as the next king. He had it made, being next in line for the throne. He was going to call the shots. People would hang on his every word, and nothing he wanted would be withheld from him.

Then, because of Saul's sin, God rejected him and directed Samuel to anoint David as king over Israel. Imagine what this meant for Jonathan. Suddenly his future was in jeopardy.

He could have done everything in his power to try to keep anyone else from stepping in to grab his place; but Jonathan's chief concern was for his nation, not for himself. He wasn't grasping for a position. He just wanted to submit to whatever strategy God devised, and he would cheerfully play whatever part God assigned him. The purity of his desire was apparent in that Jonathan not only willingly laid down his right to the throne but actually encouraged David to take the kingship. His chief joy was seeing Israel prosper; his own role was incidental.

We will never have strong churches unless we develop the Jonathan mentality. We need to draw our greatest satisfaction from the welfare of the church. Our concern for the prosperity of the church must far exceed our concern for the progress of our own ministry.

Jesus listened to His disciples argue about which of them would sit to His right and to His left. Did he encourage them to invest their time daydreaming about their positions? No. He taught them that the greatest would be the servant of all. Jesus Himself, who had the highest position of all, gave it up and came among us as the chief servant.

A refreshing change

A few years ago a group of national Christian leaders met in Denver. Many of the people there were leaders of large churches and well-known ministries. Now, when preachers get together, the natural tendency is to start comparing notes. "How big is your church?" "Where have you been invited to speak this year?" "How many radio stations are carrying you now?" I sensed, though, that many of the leaders in this gathering had grown weary of this shallow preoccupation with ministerial function.

They were on a refreshingly different wavelength: chief among their concerns was what God was doing in the church. The feeling was, "Who cares what you do? Who cares what I do? We care about what God wants for His church."

Someone's role in ministry—whether a pastor leads a very small church or a very large one, for example—says nothing about his zeal for God. God doesn't judge us by the outward appearance of success; that can be very misleading. He is concerned with the motivations of the heart.

The question everyone hears in the world is, "What do you do?" But we need to root this off-center mentality out of the church. God wants people to be consumed by their spiritual desire, not by their function within His house. *What* we do in the kingdom is far less important than *why* we do it. Our functions are so small, so temporal, compared to the eternity God wants to be set in our hearts. He wants us to be taken up with building a church that will be "the everlasting pride and the joy of all generations."[3] When we see things from that perspective, "my ministry" doesn't really matter. We forget about getting, building, and preserving our own ministries. Instead, we simply report for duty in the house of God with a willingness to do whatever needs to be done.

'Famous'

Several years ago we hired Sherrill, one of the men in our church, as our church custodian. When people went out to have pizza after an evening service, he was working—turning off the lights, adjusting the air conditioning, locking up the building. Saturday mornings, while others were climbing out of bed feeling around for their first cup of coffee, Sherrill was at church taking charge of one of the home-group cleanup crews. Sunday afternoons, when everyone went home to have dinner and take naps, he was busy rearranging chairs in a dozen Sunday-school classrooms so they would be ready for our school Monday morning.

No job is beneath him. He loves his work. Sherrill is a quiet, faithful servant, often doing mundane tasks far from the spotlight, never mentioning that he has a college degree. Years ago he saw the need for someone to take care of the physical facilities, and he was willing to fill that slot.

Sherrill has a nickname in our church. Someone once commented that Sherrill's faithful service made him famous in God's eyes. Everyone knew it was true. And the name stuck— "Famous." Sherrill does not have a high-profile position in our church, but people respect him highly. Why? Because when they look at his life they see the character of Christ; they see a man with a vision for the house of God.

The Bible exhorts us to empty ourselves, just as Jesus emptied Himself and gave up His heavenly glory with the Father. I believe that as part of that emptying process, God wants us to lay down the spiritual talents and gifts to which we can so desperately cling, that we might find our worth, security, and significance in Him alone. For some, this might mean telling God in sincere prayer that we are willing to relinquish our talents and ministry aspirations. God might ask others to walk away from their ministry for a season and become like the apostle Paul, who suffered the loss of all things that He might gain Christ.[4] God desires that we give Him all of ourselves so that He can fill us completely with His Spirit. He does not want people aspiring for ministry, because He is not building ministries; He is building the church. We are instructed to earnestly seek spiritual gifts for the *edification of the church*,[5] not for the exaltation of an individual.

Signing up to serve

Over the years I have found a simple way to sniff out the My Ministry Syndrome. It's really very easy: just give people a chance to serve. And I don't mean singing a special song on Sunday morning. I mean mopping the floors, serving meals, giving someone in a wheelchair a ride to church. If they balk, that tells you something. If they serve diligently and cheerfully, that tells you something else.

For the past several years we've hosted a conference for church leaders. This undertaking requires a lot of volunteer effort. In the midst of such labor-intensive projects, people's attitudes about ministry become readily apparent. It's greatly encouraging to see people jump in with both feet, eager to do whatever they're asked.

One man, an attorney for the state of Missouri, had been saved just a few months when he volunteered to work at the conference.

"What should I do?" he asked.

"Sign up to help," somebody suggested.

Dozens of people were needed on the kitchen and dining room crews, so he put his name down. The person in charge made him a waiter's helper. His assignment was to tag along behind the waiter and help him cart trays of food and dirty dishes. This fellow didn't think twice about it. He just wanted to help out wherever he was needed. His professional credentials made no difference; he just became one of the kitchen crew, throwing himself into the work of hauling dish tubs, scrubbing pots, scraping plates, and the like.

Our annual leadership conference has turned out to be a boot camp in the basics of servanthood. When we were first asked to host the conference, we made plans to accommodate about seventy-five church leaders. They needed transportation, housing, and meals. One attractive option was to use a convention center, where the "leave-the-hassle-to-us" hospitality pros make it their business to serve. A shuttle bus whisks guests from the airport to the hotel, and dozens of employees are on hand to make their stay effortless and enjoyable. Doormen carry bags. Maids straighten up. Waiters bring out platters of food. An unseen army vacuums the floors, wipes the counters, empties the ashtrays, and deals with soiled linen, dirty dishes, and countless other nitty-gritty chores.

But as believers, we knew that serving is supposed to be our business. And we figured that if paid hotel workers could provide more gracious hospitality to ministers of the gospel than the church could, then we needed some practice in the art of servanthood. So, practice we did. Our goal was to give "double honor"[6] to these devoted kingdom laborers by rolling out the red carpet for them. For one week we turned the church into a mini-conference center with a restaurant and shuttle service. People's homes became our guest suites.

That first gathering in 1983 has grown into an annual event that in 1988 drew leaders from sixteen states as well as Italy, England, Switzerland, Brazil, Canada, Mexico, and Sweden. From the start, the conference has been an all-hands-on-deck undertaking for our church. Many people rearrange their work schedules to be free for a day or two. Some even sacrifice a week's vacation, choosing to work at the conference rather than lounge on some sunny beach in Florida. Teens get into the act, waiting on tables or babysitting so mothers with small children can help out. In all, 300 people, including several volunteers from other churches, pitched in last year. That gave us a one-to-one ratio of guests and hosts.

This annual undertaking has taught us many lessons about serving together in God's house. People who have worked at the conferences wrote about their experiences, trying to paint a picture of behind-the-scenes ministry and what they learned from it. These stories, told by people who got down into the trenches, provide a close-up view of our life together, complete with the wrinkles and warts.

Essential ingredients

Janis, the conference's chief organizer, recalled our humble beginnings and shared some spiritual principles she has learned:

> In the beginning, it was hard to imagine how we could make lasagna for 100 with one oven, one refrigerator, and one sink. And squeezing a busy cooking crew into the church's eight-by-ten-foot kitchen was like cramming a college fraternity into a phone booth. But we did have the willing hands of people who love God

and love His family. This proved to be the most essential ingredient. Each one came with his own supply, and as we pooled our limited abilities, God's limitless possibilities began to emerge.

Sometimes fifty people would be preparing or serving a single meal. Twenty people would arrive to chop lettuce for salads. Others would be clustered around tables, peeling garlic, dicing onions, rolling meatballs, cutting out pastry. With all of us crowded together in tiny rooms, the stoves weren't the only things that got hot!

We found that people's opinions and tastes differ a great deal. Do we season with garlic? Should the punch be sweet or tangy? Should the picture hang to the left or right of the couch? We found our biggest failures could always be traced back to our attitudes. This was where our relationships faced the real test. When our attention turns from loving each other to getting our own way, disaster always seems to strike. Those are the moments that give opportunity for apology and forgiveness and make us realize our sufficiency is from God, not from ourselves.

One morning when the kitchen team met for prayer, God challenged us with the truth of 1 Corinthians 13:2-3. We could have faith to move mountains (put on a conference for several hundred people); we could feed the poor (these pastors weren't exactly rich); we could even give our bodies to be burned (at this point, most of us felt like we were in the fire); but if we didn't love one another, we were nothing. That hit home. We could serve up a hundred exquisite meals, but it was all worthless in God's sight if we didn't love one another in the process. We began to pray that as we worked together in the kitchen, our relationships would spread the "aroma" of Jesus.

Sometimes we felt totally drained. But God didn't leave us empty. As people worked together doing simple tasks—chopping vegetables, scraping dishes, scouring pans—facades came down, friendships formed, and God began to join people together. Someone would give you a heartfelt hug. Another would pass by humming praise songs as he carried out the trash. Or someone would share a scripture with such love that you knew Jesus was loving you through her.

There, in the servant's quarters, God was with us, and we praised Him for what He was doing. We could see Jesus stretching us beyond our natural abilities and drawing us together into one. And like the wedding servants who saw Jesus turn water into wine, we knew where the miracle came from.

Paper plate perfection

Ronda Kay signed up to work in the kitchen at a conference. She previously had been part of a small congregation where she had the reputation as a hard-working volunteer because she supervised the church dinners. She found herself in for a few surprises when she began serving at the conferences.

One of my first assignments was to wash lettuce— several boxes of it—for a luncheon. The lettuce leaves were to be laid on plates to make a colorful base for "fruit kabobs": skewered grapes, pineapple, and oranges.

My supervisor told me, "Save only the big, perfect leaves." So several of us sorted and washed them, then lined up rows of leaves in big plastic tubs. Then someone else came up and said, "Oh, that's too big; the leaves need to be *this* size." So we went back through the lettuce again and tore all the leaves to the prescribed

size. A while later, a third overseer came up and said, "You know, this lettuce is really wet. That will make the croissants soggy. Can you dry it?"

At this point, I was steaming. "Okay, folks," I thought to myself. "I'm thirty-three years old. I've been cooking for years. I've organized dozens of church dinners. Are you telling me I can't even wash lettuce to your standards?"

Our crew went through every one of those tubs once again, painstakingly drying each lettuce leaf on both sides with a paper towel. In the midst of it, God began convicting me about my attitude toward His house. The Lord was telling me, "You've always served Me the leftovers."

My mind went back to those many church dinners I'd organized. Planning was nonexistent. Everybody just brought what they had, and if we ran out of food, I didn't worry about it.

I thought it was a big deal to spend fifteen minutes getting things ready. People had one choice of beverage: water. I'd put a cooler out next to a stack of paper cups—whatever size happened to be in the cupboards. Paper plates were fine. And whoever happened to be last in line ran the risk of being shorted a plastic fork or spoon. I didn't bother to organize a cleanup crew. I would just go home and leave the mess to whoever stayed late.

I expected little of myself, and that's just what I got. I didn't need to lean on God to get things accomplished because I could easily do everything myself. I was content with just getting by.

But at the conference I was learning that God wants my *best* effort. The house of God is to be a place of excellence, a place where second-rate standards aren't adequate.

That first year, God was challenging me to raise my standards, to aim even higher than my own capabilities. I began to see the wisdom in that. Rather than relying on my own strength, I had to depend on God. Later on, as the challenges got tougher, I had the knowledge that unless I really prayed about what I was doing and leaned on God, it wasn't going to work.

The next year Ronda Kay signed up for kitchen duty once again and was assigned the task of making egg rolls, garlic rolls, and corn muffins:

I hadn't been in the kitchen very long when I realized I'd made a mistake by not trying out the recipes beforehand. Instead, I muddled around a long time trying to figure out what to do. That put me behind schedule and created a logjam in the kitchen. Jamie, the woman making dessert, needed the convection oven I was using. My muffins were holding her up and threatening to hold up everyone's lunch.

I fully expected Jamie to give me an icy stare that said, "Lady, you're wrecking my course!" Instead she just kept coming in to "check on me" and ask how much more time I'd need.

Then, when my cornbread came out, another mistake became apparent: I shouldn't have used the convection oven. It had caused the muffins to tilt to one side; they looked like so many elephant trunks.

I kept expecting some belittling remark, but people spared my feelings and even covered my mistakes. Somebody walking by noticed the pans and asked, "What are these?"

"They're corn muffins" was the only reply. People were making an effort not to place blame. Nobody offered me words of correction or criticism. Everybody knew I had messed up, and they figured I knew it, too.

What a difference from a worldly work place where everyone seems to lie in wait to "get you"! I learned about God's grace that year. He's not up there waiting for us to mess up; He's on our side.

Each year at the conference, I feel a little more competent but never adequate. I've found, though, that God always provides people to help cover my mistakes. As one small part of the body, I can't manage very well. God knows that, and He doesn't ask the impossible. But when the whole body joins together we can reach for excellence, and, more often than not, hit the mark.

A flash in the pan

Dan, a professional cook who has had a large role in the cooking ministry, wrote about his first day preparing meals for the conference:

I'll never forget the excitement—and the anxiety—that accompanied our church's first attempt at hosting visiting ministers. Our kitchen at that time was inadequate to feed a crowd, so we opted to cook some food in another church's kitchen and transport it back.

The first meal began with a minor disaster. Early Tuesday morning I drove to our "branch" kitchen, turned on the ovens, and went out to my car to get the meat I had brought. When I went back in the kitchen something was burning. Smoke was billowing from the oven to the ceiling. Panic-stricken, I raced to the oven, threw open the door, and pulled out two pans of flaming pine cones! I had inadvertently charred a craft project that had been left in the oven to dry. A lady standing by to make sure I didn't leave a mess in the kitchen had some reassuring words: "Boy, somebody's going to be mad when they find out about this." An auspicious beginning, indeed.

I cut the meat up, put it in the ovens, then left for work. Now, being a professional cook, I took pride in my ability to cook meat to perfection. But this time I didn't give enough instructions to the person I left in charge. Everybody's hopes were set on serving succulent roast beef, but on returning to the kitchen I found our main course had turned into several hunks of stringy leather. My co-workers lifted my sagging spirits by offering words of encouragement—no criticism. We salvaged some of the meat and ground the rest into barbecued beef.

When we loaded up the food I stuck a big pot of gravy in my trunk. Somewhere on the way home I took a sharp turn, tipped the pot, and sloshed more than a gallon of gravy all over my month-old car.

It was with this sterling effort that I began my service at the leadership conferences. Despite my lackluster performance, I was beginning to see for the first time that the members of Christ's body could work successfully together. It happened as people set aside their own preferences and pulled together for the sake of Jesus and His church. With love as our goal, our biggest "bombs" sometimes became the building blocks of our relationships.

I've seen how things work in the secular food business: people complain, resist authority, gripe about their fellow workers, and strive to show off their own talents. But if we allow Him to, God can use ministries such as the kitchen to kill the pride and selfishness that hinder our cooperation.

The late Arthur Wallis, the widely respected church leader and author from Great Britain, spoke at our leadership conference one year. He wanted to see what was happening behind the scenes, so he visited a kindergarten room that had become a makeshift kitchen. About thirty people were crowded inside. Some were cleaning up; some were eating leftovers; some were sprawled out on the floor, napping. They'd just churned out an elegant dinner for several hundred pastors and their wives.

Arthur surveyed the hubbub and said, "So this is where the action is." He looked like a small child in a candy factory. Our efforts, he told us, deeply affected him. He saw in us a living example of the body of Christ working as it was intended.

My own flaming pine cone fiasco, overdone roasts, and gravy stains are evidence enough that the success didn't come from anyone's high-level performance. Rather, it was the Lord who performed for us. He blended our strengths and weaknesses, our talents and lack of talent, and made something of which we could all be proud.

In God's house the kitchen doesn't have any superstars; but you will find plenty of servants.

CHAPTER 17

THE PARACHURCH BARRIER

While the church has remained relatively passive over the last several decades, a broad array of organizations has emerged to fill the gaps in ministry. Parachurch ministry organizations, which are set up outside the structure of the local church, are typically composed of zealous believers willing to serve on the front lines, shouldering some of the weightiest work of the church. These ministries focus on tasks such as foreign missions, campus evangelism, and literature distribution.

Such organizations dominate the scene today because the needs are so great and the church is not prepared to meet them. But as the parachurch organizations have grown strong and multiplied, this strategy of channeling resources through a system that bypasses the church has had an unforeseen result: it has actually hindered the church from regaining its strength and assuming its full responsibilities. While it is certainly not the intent of leaders of parachurch ministries to hinder the church, some of them have unwittingly promoted a mentality that deters its advancement.

God is revitalizing the church today, and I believe we need to consider making some adjustments in the strategy by which ministry is carried out. We need to reclaim a biblical pattern of ministry that elevates the local church in advancing and maintaining God's kingdom.

John the Baptist fulfilled a valuable role in ministry during a critical time in Israel's history. But once the Messiah arrived, John instructed his disciples to follow Him. "He must increase," he told them, "but I must decrease." If John had been unwilling to give way, his valuable contribution to the history of the church would have greatly diminished.

I see a like situation in the role that parachurch groups have assumed today. In the absence of vigorous ministry on the part of the church, sincere believers have done the best they could to carry out ministry through alternative means. This is certainly to their credit; much of their work has been praiseworthy. But now, we need to follow the more excellent way. Of the individual Christians involved in parachurch groups, I believe that those who discern God's focus in the world today will choose to join forces with their brethren in the local church. Sadly, I believe that those who do not recognize the desire of God to restore the church will end up as part of the parachurch barrier.

Out of the bleachers

In televised football games, the cameras periodically cut away from the action on the gridiron and show an aerial view of the stadium. From the vantage point of the Goodyear blimp, it's obvious the playing field is mostly empty—only about two dozen scattered specks of color are visible. But surrounding the field is a huge bowl of colorful humanity: tens of thousands of people packed together in the bleachers, shouting their encouragement and cheering on the few who are part of the action far below on the field.

Many of us have received letters from Christian organizations that say something like this: "We're involved in a vital ministry that needs your help. Please send a check today." Whether the appeal is made in a newsletter, a magazine, or on a radio or television broadcast, the theme tends to be essentially the same. Those appeals go out by the millions to a scattered flock of believers throughout the world who serve as the "congregations" of parachurch ministries. These are the people in the grandstands; they support their favorite teams by sending money in response to the appeals they choose to heed. With their attention fixed on a few high profile ministers who make the big plays, they join the millions scattered in local churches who are satisfied with watching the action rather than participating in it.

Commendable zeal

I'm not saying this to criticize the parachurch ministries or the people involved with them. These people are working in the inner cities, running homes for pregnant teens, ministering to drug addicts, sending music groups and athletic teams abroad to share the gospel. They travel around the globe to build schools, run clinics, and publish literature. Of course, these endeavors cost money, and the ministry organizations need to generate substantial sums to support these worthy projects.

These works excite believers who have a passion to serve God. Many of them hear about these ministries and decide to sign up themselves. They then take their places on the playing field, and turn to their friends in the "stands," the church, for support. Countless believers in the local churches then remain largely inactive, watching the action from a distance. They hear about the trials and triumphs of those laboring in ministry. They hear about the unbelievers others are converting, the responses to prayer others are seeing, the miracles others are witnessing. By all reports, the action is exciting down on the field. But what about all those people up in the stands? Is Christianity supposed to be a spectator sport—just plunk down your money, buy a ticket, take your seat, and applaud? Unwittingly, the parachurch configuration has promoted an approach to Christianity that leaves the average believer inactive. He may provide support, but he's not challenged to step onto the playing field. In a healthy local church, everyone is called to be on the playing field, serving in some way.

What role for the church?

Investing our efforts in ministries that emerge from a strong local church may not seem quite as invigorating as traveling the world with a parachurch evangelistic team. It is, however, a much more active role than just mailing in checks or supplies to front-line troops. And, most importantly, we need to consider what role it is that God wants us to fill. Are we just to sit by and watch others carry the ball, or are we to be down on the playing field in our own local churches?

Jerry White, general director of The Navigators, wrote about the Christian spectator mentality. This is an excerpt from an article in his organization's *Discipleship Journal* magazine:

> A generation raised on thrilling movies, dynamic television programs, and professional sports becomes bored with "ordinary" church. The demand for platform entertainment, exciting programs and stellar preaching seems far removed from those small bands of early Christians. Commitment—the call to be a part of a local body of believers, for better or worse—is a foreign concept to many Christians today.[1]

White goes on to challenge believers to become involved personally in a local congregation, calling such involvement "imperative":

> Can one be a committed disciple and not be a part of a local congregation? Practically, I believe the answer is no. If we take the Scriptures seriously, committed discipleship must include fellowship, interaction, and functioning with other believers.[2]

Christians don't hear much talk like this, stressing the importance of being committed to a local church. It's rare to hear a Christian radio or television broadcast encourage people to tithe or make significant monetary contributions to their own churches. Instead, because of their own financial pressures, they're forced to issue frequent requests for support to keep their own ministries going.

But what would happen if all the people in the stands were down on the playing field? What would happen if there were no spectators, if every believer was devoting his best efforts to advancing the kingdom in his own local church?

A visit with Keith Green

One of the most zealous Christians I have ever met was the late Keith Green, the musician who founded Last Days Ministries. I had great respect for Keith; to me and to the others he touched through his ministry, he represented a man totally sold out to God.

Keith came to visit several times. We would stay up into the early hours of the morning, arguing with feverish intensity, as friends do at times, over our convictions. One of these conversations was particularly memorable. We stayed up the entire night debating an issue on which we couldn't come to terms. Keith was on fire for what he was doing with his Last Days Ministries, and he couldn't understand why I was pastoring a church in Columbia, Missouri, when I could be doing something *really* significant in the kingdom. He couldn't see how anybody with zeal for God, a heart for ministry, and a global vision would want to stay in a church. He felt his strategy would be far more effective in reaching the millions who need the gospel.

I'm not knocking Keith for this. The truth is, he had a point. In the system we have grown up with, the church is the place from which we expect the "good students" to graduate to a higher level of commitment and service.

The biblical pattern

We have managed to move so far in the parachurch direction that it's difficult to get back on the local church track. But it's clear that the New Testament pattern shows us something quite different from the structure of much of Christian ministry today. There were no parachurch ministries in the New Testament. When famine struck Jerusalem, no world-hunger relief organization was on hand to send supplies. Instead, the churches in Greece took up a collection to provide food for their brethren across the Mediterranean.[3]

In New Testament times, evangelism and foreign missions were not relegated to independent organizations. These projects were undertaken by strong local churches, such as the powerful bodies in Antioch and Jerusalem. The churches equipped the saints, commissioning apostles, prophets, teachers, and evangelists; and through the guidance of the Holy Spirit they sent out missionary teams, such as Paul and Barnabas, to preach the gospel and establish and strengthen local churches. Without the benefit of modern technology or transportation, the churches of the New Testament launched a powerful assault against the forces of darkness. In the course of a single generation they planted a network of churches in villages and cities across several continents, establishing a beachhead for Christianity that fundamentally changed the moral and spiritual climate of much of the world and laid the foundation of Western civilization. How's that for potential?

This same pattern, which is not only more effective but also far more efficient, needs to be duplicated in our day.

Labor drain

There are two very practical ways the parachurch structure hinders the work of the local church. First, parachurch organizations, which tend to be seen as the crack corps of ministry, attract the sharpest, most committed men and women. Rather than these bright young servants digging in and fulfilling the call of God on their lives right in their own churches, they are more inclined to heed the call of a parachurch group that fits their ministry direction. I have seen this happen over and over myself, and have listened to many a frustrated pastor who has watched the "cream of the crop" in his flock head off for greener ministry pastures.

One young woman in a church in England who had a heart for evangelism had brought many new people into her local church. She was fired up about sharing the gospel, and she talked to the pastor about enrolling in an evangelism training school offered by a parachurch organization. The pastor agreed. She asked the church to help pay for her schooling and cover the cost of a ministry trip to the Soviet Union, which followed the training program. The church covered half the cost, and individuals and home groups pitched in additional funds, so the church's total investment ran into thousands of dollars. The pastor explains what happened when this fervent evangelist returned.

> She came back to the church, and the team shared how they got on in Russia, and it was quite fun, quite exciting. And if that wasn't exciting enough, she came back to see me the following day and said, "I've been praying a lot about this. The team has been praying a lot about this, and we don't feel I should come back to our church."

She had decided to join the parachurch group. And, once again, she turned to her friends in the church for financial support, and they provided it. The pastor lamented this woman's departure because it dealt a significant blow to his church.

> It threw us. We lost her, one of our sparkling jewels who really reached out and drew others into the church. We missed her a lot. What really happened was we had been bled of one of our sparks for outreach. That's a loss. It's not a small loss. It's a big loss.

Rather than harness her zeal to help build the church in her own community, this woman "graduated" from the local church and took her desires and abilities elsewhere. This scenario, sadly enough, has become a normal pattern in the church today.

A few years ago, we invited a traveling Christian drama troupe to perform at our church. The performers put on a musical production as an evangelistic outreach to the community and gave several nightly performances. Our church has its own drama ministry, which has also put on some productions for the community; and while this drama troupe was visiting, they tried to recruit our talented theater people to join their ministry. Rather than encouraging them to excel in what they were already doing in the church, they urged them to leave.

Another incident illustrating this talent drain on the church occurred when one of the men in our church heard about a European mission group that was seeking someone with computer expertise to help in its main office. He had experience with computers and was intrigued by this international ministry, so he came in one day to talk things over with me. This man is a solid believer, zealous for God, and active in ministry. Those qualities make him a valuable part of our church; they also made him an excellent prospect for that mission group. He could have had the job with the group. There was one hitch, though: he would need to raise his own support—enough money for air fare to Europe and money to live on in his new home. He laid out the situation for me, and I thought about what this ministry was offering him.

"I'll make you a counter-offer," I told him, half-seriously. "You can come to work here—on the same terms. We won't cover your expenses or give you a salary, but you can work full time in ministry."

I told him that in my view we, too, have an international ministry. People in our church are reaching out to foreign students from Asia, Africa, and the Far East on the university campus. Some students who have become Christians here have gone back home, and we still hear reports about how they are zealously building God's church in Japan, Nigeria, Peru, and other nations. We have sent construction crews to spend a few weeks building churches in Central and South America. We support native missionaries in India. One of our leaders and his wife are working in Brazil, serving as house-parents in a church-run orphanage. And we're building ties with the leaders of local churches in Europe, South America, Asia, and Africa.

So, if this man was looking to be part of a group that would touch other nations, he didn't need to look any further. And as far as responding to needs, our church could use some technical help with computers, too. I think the process of thinking through his opportunity helped the man expand even further his vision of what the local church can do. Much to my delight he is still here, working hard in the church as a home-group leader.

When people leave the church to pursue their ministry ambitions, the church is given a blow. Some of the church's best workers disappear out of the local church's labor force. Does this mean that no one should ever leave a local church? Definitely not. But there are several issues that are good to consider before leaving the local church: Leaving to go where? And to do what? Is God wanting to build ministries or churches?

Misdirected funds

While losing zealous young believers drains the church of its most productive workers, the church loses out on another significant front. Millions and millions of dollars that could have been dropped into local church offering baskets go instead to parachurch ministries to fund their activities. The result is that the church is further debilitated, left without the resources to carry out the kinds of ministries that emerged from New Testament churches like that of Antioch.

A church in Kansas had a family whose father had lost his job. He had been out of work for some time when his son got hurt and ended up in the hospital. The day came when the family didn't even have enough money to buy groceries. This crisis hit at the same time a parachurch ministry experienced a financial crunch of its own. Here the pastor of that church tells how one man in his congregation reacted to these developments.

Several people came to me about this family's needs, and through the church grapevine it was well known that this family had a great financial need.

One fellow, who I'm sure was aware of this family's situation, came up to me and said he had received a letter from a TV evangelist with a plea for money. He said that if he didn't have so many dollars before a particular time, his ministry couldn't stay on the air.

This church member wanted the pastor to make a public announcement encouraging the congregation to contribute to the TV evangelist's ministry. The pastor turned him down without hesitation. The incident highlighted for him the frustration of having parachurch ministries in financial competition with the local church. Here he describes a disturbing mentality he finds too often in the church:

> People want to invest their finances in something that makes them feel bigger than themselves. In investing in those close to us, we don't get that "high" that we would get from investing in somebody who holds crusades in which thousands come to Christ. People tend to think that somehow they're getting more for their money. They think the guy sitting next to them is insignificant in the overall picture, and that if he goes under or leaves the church, that doesn't have nearly as much [significance] as if a TV evangelist went under.
>
> Too many people in the church see themselves as not doing anything that's really significant in the world. They're just performing religious duties. They see these other guys working for Jesus as the really spiritual ones. We think that people like us—the average guy in the church—can be replaced. But we think the "superstars" are one in million.

That is the mentality that produces a money drain on the church, leaving its leaders unable to meet the needs at home.

A pastor I know encountered an unexpected financial crisis in his church a few years ago. This hardship made him as desperate for funds as parachurch ministries frequently say they are. The bank had threatened to foreclose on the building, and the church needed to raise tens of thousands of dollars very quickly. He explains what happened:

> Because our church believed in missions, we had supported approximately twenty-two parachurch ministries outside our church for about four years. I felt as though the Holy Spirit gave me the idea to write a letter—it was about a two-page letter—explaining the crisis that we had in our church. In fact, the letter I constructed was very much like the letters I had been receiving for years from these ministries. It told of a real need we had in our church: we were afraid we were going to lose our building. I didn't send the letter just to the twenty-two ministries we supported—I sent a total of forty-eight letters to different parachurch ministries.
>
> Out of forty-eight letters, we received money from two of them—one gift of $100, and one gift of $1,000. Ironically, the one that sent us $1,000 was one that we had previously sent $1,000. The other responses I got said, "We do not send money ouside of our ministry."
>
> One letter enclosed a tract on how to plant seeds and receive a harvest. Another form letter from [the same] group, asking for money, came about three weeks later. I had to laugh.
>
> I felt like it was one-sided. The attitude is, "You give to us. You're just a local church, but we're something important."

That pastor's disappointment caused him to reevaluate his church's strategy, and it sparked within him a greater commitment to the local church.

Starving at the storehouse

To understand more about this money drain and its implications for the church, I'd like to explore a section of the Bible that clarifies the issue of who is to be the recipient of our tithes and offerings.

The last part of the book of Malachi issues a rebuke to the Israelites for failing to follow the Lord's instructions on giving. God had told the Israelites to bring the entire tithe and offering into the storehouse. Since the people were failing to do that, God accused them of actually robbing Him. Those are pretty strong words. But in His mercy He does provide them with a way to return to His favor:

> "Bring all the tithes into the storehouse, that there may be food in My house, and prove Me now in this," says the Lord of hosts, "if I will not open for you the windows of heaven and pour out for you such blessing that there will not be room enough to receive it."[4]

The storehouse represents the designated gathering place for the people of God. I think it's scripturally accurate to conclude that the local church is to be today's storehouse.[5] If the church is going to be strong, we must bring our tithes and offerings into it. If we fail to entrust our local church leaders with the funds we give to God, we are circumventing the key strategy prescribed in the Bible for supplying ministry to a needy world.

Avoiding Abraham's mistake

It's easy to understand the motivation for launching parachurch organizations. We look at a small local church and think, "What could that weak little group do?" But remember Abraham and Sarah. When God gave them the promise that Sarah would bear a son, they were both old, well past the age when people bear and raise children. In coming up with their own plan to start a family, Abraham and Sarah made the same mistake people make today when they say the local church can never amount to anything, and give their support instead to parachurch groups.

Coming to an end is the era in which Christians drop a few dollars in the church offering plate, then write substantial checks to various parachurch ministries. Those who have this approach to giving will never build a strong church; they have a big vision for what the parachurch ministries can accomplish and a small vision for the local church. Not only is that way of thinking erroneous, it's also inefficient. It's time to adjust our strategy.

Turning the tide

Whenever I hear financial appeals from ministries outside the church, my response is always the same: "I'm just as zealous about my cause as you are about yours. I'm investing everything I have in my cause. And, just like you, I share my burden with anyone who will listen."

In a parachurch ministry magazine, a well-known evangelist made this statement: "Whoever gets to the local church first will win the race in the 1990s."[6] He went on to suggest that churches and parachurch ministries should band together in an evangelism partnership. "Parachurch organizations could supply the evangelistic mindset and expertise," he said, "and churches could provide prayer, financial support, and volunteers."

Here is the partnership he envisions: the parachurch groups have the strategy and wisdom; the church has the money and the manpower. I often get several calls a month from various ministries whose survival depends on this "partnership." They are always surprised to discover that our church has a vision of its own, a vision that requires all our time, our money, our zeal. My perspective is that God calls each local church to a vision that will consume its resources.

Speaking as a pastor, I have at times felt the pressure of guil
applied by some who wanted access to the congregation. The
seemed to feel that I was partially responsible for their support
since they were pursuing an independent ministry. We've al
heard the appeals of the evangelists who say, "If I don't hea
from you today, my ministry is finished." My question is this
why am I responsible for the demise of someone else's ministry
Who do they think has set them into these positions—me o
God?

The rhetoric of the fund-raising world centers around faith
Individuals and groups are "believing God" for support. But i
reality, the fund-raising techniques are too often manipulativ
and even exploitative. The implication is that if I don't suppor
what they want to do, I am responsible to God for their failure
These techniques must end.

I'm working for the day when millions of believers will pou
their zeal and energy, their time and their funds, into loca
churches with community-changing, nation-changing, and worlc
changing vision. To me, that is a worthy cause.

This perspective has not developed simply because I am
pastor. My conviction is that everyone in the local church—th
janitor, the Sunday school teacher, the teenager, the mother c
six—can have the same fervent spirit of a Keith Green. God feel
great passion for His church, and when someone is part of a loca
church he is part of something extremely significant. Believer
do not belong on the sidelines rooting for somebody on the fielc
they belong in the middle of the action in their own churche
And whether their job is running the lights in a drama productior
programming a computer, cleaning up the nursery, raising
family, or teaching a Bible study, like Jesus, they can b
consumed with zeal for the house of God.

A change in the offing

God's Spirit is moving across the earth and awakening within Hi
people a passion to see the church become the praise of th

earth. In churches across the world, the Spirit is sovereignly restoring a vision for the house of God. As this process continues, as local churches arise and begin taking their rightful place, there will be less and less need for substitutes to fill the gap. The drain of people and funds from the church will diminish, and more of people's devotion and more of their resources will be available for ministry in the local church. God will raise up the magnificent church He has promised and so make way for even more fruitful ministry in which every Christian assumes his proper place. As this happens, we will see believers leaving their seats in the bleachers and charging onto the playing field. This is the more excellent way.

CHAPTER 18

DEVOTED
TO A CAUSE

My Uncle Louie told me he was convinced there was a God. I asked him how he knew for sure.

"I saw him in Pennsylvania," he said.

"Pennsylvania?" I asked, wondering if he was leading into some sort of joke.

"Yes, Pennsylvania. I was driving there, looking at the colors of the leaves and the hills. Then at night I looked at all the stars in the sky, and I said to myself, 'Only God could make all this.'"

Many of us have had a similar experience. Even someone like me, not known for artistic sensitivity and a love of the great outdoors, cannot escape sensing the divine artistry in nature.

Inner awareness

Everyone gains an inner awareness of God through the tangible things He has made. A sparkling mountain stream, the autumn splendor of an Appalachian forest, and the wonder of the Grand Canyon all resound with the clear message: there is a God in heaven.

The Bible says as much:

For since the creation of the world God's invisible qualities—his eternal power and divine nature—have been clearly seen, being understood from what has been made, so that men are without excuse.[1]

God is invisible to us. His power, His wisdom, His love cannot be seen. Yet He has not left the world without a visible reflection of Himself. Everyone who observes God's creation—whether through a telescope, seeing its vastness, or through a microscope, seeing its intricate details, has ample evidence of the Creator's presence. Only a fool, the Bible says, would say there is no God.[2]

Soaring peaks, glimmering stars

Jesus said He would create something else on the earth, something even more majestic than the mountains, something that would shine brighter than the stars. Something that would provide even more powerful evidence of His presence in the world.

"I will build My church," He said, "and the gates of hell shall not prevail against it." Just as my uncle knew that God is real because of what he saw in nature, people will say, "I know Jesus is real because I saw Him in the church."

The church, specifically bodies of believers assembled in local communities, is the only group of people with the potential to express God's character. Why? Because God Himself is creating it. It is not to be a political nation, an economic system, or a religious institution. None of those would express His nature clearly. Only the church, God's family who loves Him and love one another, can express His nature to a world hungry for reality.

As believers it is critical that we understand the significance of our life together in the local church. Our relationships form a testimony more powerful than soaring mountain peaks or a million glimmering stars. God wants our lives to "shine like stars in the universe."[3] He wants us to ascend toward heaven as the "mountain of the Lord." Like the stars and the mountains, He wants us to be an accurate expression of His purpose for human life.

Unfortunately, the glimmer of the stars is shrouded by confusion. The majesty of the Lord's mountain is tarnished by failure and weakness. Our message to the world has not been that clear representation of God's character that would draw men to Him.

But God has given us a picture of what He wants us to become—a family. He does not permit us the option of selecting our own interpretation of the Bible's picture; His instructions are clear. He has not established relationships as the means to an end, but as the end itself, the very goal God is pursuing. The evidence in Scripture for God desiring a family is overwhelming; it is not a controversial doctrine requiring scholarly skills to comprehend. The Bible presents a clear picture of what God wants.

Goliath-size barriers

Even when we see the picture of the family God wants us to become, we cannot help but notice the immense barriers barring our passage, barriers such as our careers, our possessions, our geographical preferences, our self-centeredness. These obstacles seem to ensure that the church will never achieve its destiny, never emulate the masterpiece God has painted to show us His desire. These are indeed Goliath-sized barriers, and the only way to face them is with David-like faith.

But for many of us, when we assess the state of the church, we conclude that the situation is beyond hope. The city of God lies in ruins, and its restoration will require a miracle.

Nehemiah faced such a day, when the city he dearly loved was reduced to rubble. Once a beautiful city, Jerusalem had been overrun by Babylonian invaders. This city, home of the revered temple of King Solomon, had been a place of palaces and prosperity. But the attacking army broke through the stone walls guarding the city, and with this last line of defense lost, the capital of Judah was sacked, the temple destroyed. The nation was forced to resettle hundreds of miles away.

The Babylonian exile represents one of Israel's darkest periods. They were a defeated people, foreigners and slaves, objects of scorn and derision. The exiles endured this disgrace for seventy years. Then, at last, they saw deliverance. The Persian army swept in and defeated their captors. The new government allowed 50,000 Israelites to return to their native land.

God chose Nehemiah, an influential Jew in service to the Persian king, to spearhead the work of restoration. Messengers brought him the distressing report that the walls of Jerusalem were torn down, the gates burned with fire, leaving the city defenseless. He broke down and wept, mourning for many days. His greatest desire was to restore the honor of Jerusalem. The Persian king sent him back with his blessing, even appointing him as governor of the surrounding region.

When Nehemiah arrived in Jerusalem, he found, to his dismay, that his horse could not even make its way through the barriers: heaps of burnt timber and strewn rock. For Nehemiah and the people of God, the job of clearing the debris and rebuilding miles of wall must have seemed an impossible task. But stirred by the promise of what God wanted to accomplish, Nehemiah issued a challenge to the people:

> You see the distress that we're in, how Jerusalem lies waste and the gates are burned with fire," he said. "Come, let us build up the wall of Jerusalem, that we might be no more a reproach."[4]

As he shared the vision God gave him, the people were inspired to rise up and build against all odds. The project consumed all their time and resources, and they had to fight those who tried to keep them from the task, working with one hand and holding a sword in the other. Yet the people of God were not daunted. Amid the harrassment and threats, they pressed on, "working with all their heart." The result was in God's hands, and they finished the work. Historians tell us the walls they constructed were nine feet thick and ran for more than six and a half miles. The job was completed in only fifty-two days.

Nehemiah's account is a miracle story, a story of God's people triumphing against overwhelming odds. The rebuilt walls represented something of great spiritual significance for the people of Jerusalem. Their honor was restored, their strength reestablished, and their hope for the future secured. The presence of God was felt once again. The law was understood. And the Scripture says their joy was heard from afar.

Desperate straits

Our day is like that of Nehemiah. In the face of bleak circumstances, many of us believe God will again, as He did in Nehemiah's day, restore the walls of Jerusalem. We believe that the honor, the dignity, the power of the people of God will be reestablished. We are awaiting the day when God will clear the rubble of confused doctrines and man-made methods and move the church forward toward its destiny.

Gideon faced equally grim circumstances.[5] Armies from the east had invaded Israel like swarms of locusts and had camped in the Valley of Jezreel. Gideon had 33,000 men, but the Lord told him to thin out his troops. Let anyone go home who is afraid, He said. Twenty-two thousand left, but the Lord wanted still more men sent home so Israel could not boast that her own strength had saved her. When the final cut was made, Gideon had 300 men to deploy against 135,000.

Gideon stepped into battle facing odds of 450 to 1. But Gideon's 300 carried with them a promise: their nation would succeed. With that promise fueling their faith, they overcame the odds and overwhelmed the enemy.

The promise

When God gives us a glimpse of what He has in store for us as the church, we react like Sarah, laughing at the thought of fulfilling God's promise that she would be the mother of nations. Little has changed. God still presents us with a humanly impossible challenge and asks us to have faith that He will supply a miracle. The kind of church God wants is impossible for man to build or sustain. In fact, everything that accomplishes God's purpose is solely dependent on His Spirit for its creation and growth.

So the question for us is this: Can we believe a shepherd boy can slay a giant with a slingshot? Can we believe 300 men can rout an army of 135,000? Can we believe a ninety-year-old woman can bear a son? Can God perform miracles?

Gideon was flanked by 300 men—and a promise. David was armed with a slingshot—and a promise. Sarah faced her childbearing future with a barren womb—and a promise.

Now we, the Israel of God, the family pictured on God's painting, face equally grim circumstances. We appear to be outmanned and set up for a massacre. Our opponents, like powerful giants, mock us. We hope to give birth to a church, but our womb appears barren. So what are we left with? What can offer us the hope of a successful future as a church?

We have a promise. We have the same promise that David, Gideon, and Sarah had. We can have the same confidence that in the end, though a miracle is required, it will be our troops that remain standing, our womb that gives life, our weapons that slay the giants.

Today's challenge

In a day when the local church, that family that tangibly expresses the heart of God in a community, faces the Goliath-like barriers that threaten to separate the nation from its destiny, what will be your cry?

If David were with us today, I believe you would find him exhorting his friends to embrace the promise, stake their lives on the certain destiny of God's nation, and throw themselves into the life of the local church. He would challenge us to tear down barriers and gaze ever more closely at the masterpiece of the ages that God is composing with the lives of believers through every generation.

Like David, may we be a people who will rise up in our day, recognize the promise of God in our generation, align ourselves with our brothers and sisters in the local church and call to all who will hear: *Is there not a cause?*

Appendix

A VISION
OF VICTORY

Church historian Iain Murray conducted extensive research on the vision of the future of the church embraced by our spiritual forefathers in England and early America. He presents a thoroughly documented and fascinating account in his book, *The Puritan Hope: Revival and the Interpretation of Prophecy.* He summarizes here the Puritan perspective:

> With the apostle Paul, the Puritans delighted to celebrate the truth that the power which is "able to do exceeding abundantly above all that we ask or think," is to be exercised to his glory "in the church by Christ Jesus throughout all ages, world without end" (Eph. 3:21). The Church is focal in God's eternal design to bring glory to his Son. This concept inspired the passion with which the Puritans and Covenanters threw themselves into the work of Church reformation, and it also lay behind international concern for the unity of the Church in doctrine and discipline. Their piety had a strong *corporate* emphasis; for the individualistic type of evangelical living they had no sympathy whatsoever.
>
> It should be at once apparent that this viewpoint, connected with Puritan belief on unfulfilled prophecy,

differs markedly in its practical effects from the view
which, based on another scheme of prophetic
interpretation, sees no future for the organized Church.
The Puritans saw the church as a divine institution. . .
sufficient by [God's] blessing for the full realization in
history of the promise that Christ "shall have dominion
also from sea to sea, and from the river unto the ends
of the earth" (Psa. 72:8). If the Church is the God-
appointed means for the advancement of the kingdom,
then her future is beyond all doubt. "Unto this catholic,
visible church," says the Westminster Confession,
"Christ hath given the ministry, oracles, and ordinances
of God, for the gathering and perfecting of the saints
in this life, to the end of the world; and doth by his own
presence and Spirit, according to his promise, make
the effectual thereunto."[1]

With this belief in the Church's future the Puritans
gained energy and resolution. Had they adopted the
short-term view the problems of the Church in their
day might justifiably have seemed hopeless, but they
faced them with an unflinching sense of their duty
towards posterity. Succeeding centuries would reap
the advantage of an uncompromised witness to the
Word of God. Their work could not be in vain for the
testimony of Christ's Church was yet to encircle the
world. Jonathan Edwards was to epitomize this forward-
look when he wrote, "It may be hoped that then many
of the Negroes and Indians will be divines, and that
excellent books will be published in Africa, in Ethiopia,
in Tartary."[2] The Church, after all, would be victorious![3]

In his early life, Murray himself wasn't a believer in the
"Puritan hope." In the opening pages of his book, he recalls
listening with discomfort as his father prayed for the "universal
spread and global triumph" of the kingdom of God on earth. His
father envisioned a day when multitudes in every nation would
follow Christ. To Murray, that kind of thinking was misguided

liberalism, an unscriptural view of the ability of man to improve his fallen condition. He believed that the correct evangelical view was that man's depravity would produce an ever-darkening world in which growing evil would predominate until the Second Coming.

Seeking to gain a biblical perspective on the matter, Murray studied Scripture in depth, and read extensively in works of scholarly predecessors in the faith. Here he tells how he began reconsidering his views:

> In the urging of his petitions I realized that my father was often employing scriptural language. I conceived his mistake to be that he was applying to this age and to the present course of history what is descriptive of a period which is to follow the return of Christ. Only after his personal appearing will multitudes—including the Jews as a nation—enter his kingdom; only then will ensue an age of peace when "the earth shall be full of the knowledge of the Lord, as the waters cover the sea."
>
> With this view of the future one can both believe in the present progress of evil and in a period yet to dawn when the predicted prosperity of the kingdom of God in the world will at last become a reality. In consequence one must also believe that the conclusion of this present age is not to witness the end of the world but the return of Christ and the ushering in of a new era— often called "the millennium." When that has run its course, the last judgment shall take place and time shall be no more.
>
> In accepting this outlook upon the future—an outlook which has been known as millenarianism—I was unaware of an objection which has long been urged against it. It is an objection which can be simply stated: the return of Jesus Christ is represented in the New Testament in terms which exclude the possibility

of a new era intervening between his coming and the end of the world. His second advent and "the end" will occur together (1 Cor. 15:23,24). He is to remain in heaven, not until the commencement of a millennium, but until "the time of the restoration of all things" (Acts 3:21), elsewhere spoken of as "the regeneration," which Jesus identifies with the last judgment (Matt. 19:28). When he comes all the dead will be raised, Christians glorified, the kingdom complete and the day of God's longsuffering towards sinners will be over. The witness of many texts which speak of these truths renders impossible the idea that Christ's appearing can be connected with, or followed by, a new era of spiritual blessing for those hitherto unsaved. For this reason all the Confessional statements of the Reformed Churches four hundred years ago refused to identify millenarianism with historic Christianity and spoke rather of the return of Jesus Christ as coincident with the day of judgment. The Thirty-Nine Articles declare, in connection with the resurrection of Christ, that he ascended into heaven "and there sitteth, until he return to judge all men at the last day." The Scottish Confession of Faith (1560), The Belgic Confession (1561) and the Heidelberg Catechism (1563) all repeat the same truth. "We believe, according to the Word of God, when the time appointed by the Lord (which is unknown to all creatures) is come, and the number of the elect complete, that our Lord Jesus Christ will come from heaven, corporally and visibly, as he ascended with great glory and majesty, to declare himself Judge of the quick and the dead, burning this old world with fire and flame to cleanse it. And then all men will personally appear before this great Judge, both men and women and children, that have been from the beginning of the world to the end thereof."[4]

Thus I came to see that there is an insuperable

objection to the view of prophecy which I had accepted in my early Christian life. I retain my respect and affection for those who have held and still hold that view; I know also that they urge Scripture to support it, but, when Scripture is alleged against Scripture, it is of cardinal importance that the dependence we place upon texts which are obscure in meaning or capable of more than one sense should be less than that which we place upon doctrinal texts where the sense is clear and confirmed by parallel scriptures. As the *Westminster Confession* says, "All things in scripture are not alike plain in themselves, nor alike clear unto all." Therefore, in view of the total absence of supporting evidence from the New Testament, it is exceedingly hazardous to claim that a thousand years intervene between Christ's coming and the end of the world on the grounds that Revelation 20 teaches a millennium. The truth is that Revelation 20 contains what has been called "the darkest passage in all the Bible"; widely differing meanings have been given to it by those who share a common faith in the inerrancy of Scripture, and it is better to admit that our view of that difficult chapter is uncertain rather than to commit ourselves to an interpretation which can only be harmonized with the remainder of Scripture by introducing confusion in the meaning of many passages otherwise clear.

In reply to this plea that one should begin with the plain, not the obscure, and build upon what is written large in the Word of God, it may be asked who is to decide what is "plain"? Ultimately every Christian must form his own judgment, but in this area it is wise to consider what has been the consensus of Christian opinion in the past. When, for example, we read the same testimony in the Nicene Creed of the fourth century—"He shall come again, with glory, to judge

the living and the dead"—as in the Confessions of the
Reformation—all professing that Christ's advent is the
final judgment—there ought to be strong evidence
before we conclude that this belief does not represent
the clear witness of the New Testament.[5]

Murray goes on to explain that his views on the future of the
church were also influenced by his study of the great historic
revivals of the church:

> One common reason for believing that the world
> must grow worse and worse has always been the
> evidence of abounding moral decay. Confronted by
> this evidence it has too often been supposed that the
> only work left for God is judgment. Yet the history of
> revivals should teach us that even in the midst of
> prevailing evil it is possible to form precisely the
> opposite conviction. For example, when John Wesley
> arrived in Newcastle-upon-Tyne in May, 1742, he
> wrote these memorable words: "I was surprised; so
> much drunkenness, cursing and swearing (even from
> the mouths of little children) do I never remember to
> have seen and heard before in so small a compass of
> time. Surely this place is ripe for Him who 'came not
> to call the righteous, but sinners to repentance.' "[6] And
> the great evangelical revival which was then dawning
> proved this conviction to be right. The gospel of grace
> does not need promising conditions to make its
> reception a certainty. Such a result depends upon the
> will of him who declares his love to the ungodly. Thus
> in various centuries revivals of apostolic Christianity
> have broken out in the most improbable circumstances
> and have powerfully, rapidly and extensively affected
> whole communities. "When the enemy shall come in
> like a flood, the Spirit of the Lord shall lift up a standard
> against him" (Isa. 59:19). The wonder of God's saving

works ought therefore to make Christians slow to believe that only doom and catastrophe must await the vast population of this evil earth. If, as men predict, the world population is to double in the next thirty years, why should it not be that God is going to show on a yet greater scale that truth is more powerful than error, grace more powerful than sin, and that those given to Christ are indeed "as the sand which is upon the sea-shore" for multitude?[7]

"The greatest spiritual endeavours and achievements [are] those energized by faith and hope."[8] The essence of a Christian outlook based on faith and hope, the spirit of a people caught up in God's purpose for His church, are portrayed in this passage by J. H. Thornwell, a Puritan theologian who in 1871 called on his generation to embrace a bigger vision of the church:

If the Church could be aroused to a deeper sense of the glory that awaits her, she would enter with a warmer spirit into the struggles that are before her. Hope would inspire ardor. She would even now arise from the dust, and like the eagle, plume her pinions for loftier flights than she has yet taken. What she wants, and what every individual Christian wants, is faith—faith in her sublime vocation, in her Divine resources, in the presence and efficacy of the Spirit that dwells in her—faith in the truth, faith in Jesus, and faith in God. With such a faith there would be no need to speculate about the future. That would speedily reveal itself. It is our unfaithfulness, our negligence and unbelief, our low and carnal aims, that retard the chariot of the Redeemer. The Bridegroom cannot come until the Bride has made herself ready. Let the Church be in earnest after greater holiness in her own members, and in faith and love undertake the conquest of the world, and she will soon settle the question whether her resources are competent to change the face of the earth.[9]

Notes

1. *Westminster Confession*, chapter 25, para. 3, as cited in *The Puritan Hope*. Excerpts from *Puritan Hope,* Banner of Truth Trust, Edinburgh, 1971, used by permission of the publisher.

2. *The Works of Jonathan Edwards*, 1840, vol. 1, 609, as cited in *The Puritan Hope*, p. 97

3. Murray, *Puritan Hope*, p. 96-97

4. The Belgic Confession, Article 37, *The Creeds of the Evangelical Protestant Churches*, edited by H.B. Smith and P. Schaff, 1877, 433, as cited in *Puritan Hope*, p. xvii.

5. Murray, *Puritan Hope*, p. xvi-xviii.

6. *The Journal of the Rev. John Wesley*, Standard Edition, vol. 3, 13, as cited in *Puritan Hope*, p. xx.

7. Murray, *Puritan Hope*, p. xix-xx.

8. Murray, *Puritan Hope*, p. xxii.

9. J.H. Thornwell, *Collected Writings*, 1871, vol. 2, 48, as cited in *Puritan Hope*, p. xxii.

NOTES

Preface

1. Sam. 17:29 (NKJV)

Chapter 1

1. "The Times They Are A-Changin'," Bob Dylan, M. Witmark and Son ©1963, Columbia Records 1964.
2. "San Francisco (Be Sure to Wear Some Flowers in Your Hair)," John Phillips, ©1967 Epic Records.
3. Hal Lindsey with C.C. Carlson, *The Late Great Planet Earth*, Zondervan Publishing House: Grand Rapids, Michigan, 1970.
4. David Wilkerson, *The Vision*, Pyramid Communications, Inc., 1974, p. 34.
5. Wilkerson, *The Vision*, p. 35
6. Wilkerson, *The Vision*, p. 39.
7. Willard Cantelon, *The Day the Dollar Dies*, Logos International, 1973, p. 72.
8. "I Wish We'd All Been Ready," Larry Norman, J.C. Love Publishing Co. ©1969, and Beechwood Music Corp.1972.

Chapter 2

1. Matt. 7:16
2. *Called Out* magazine, Cityhill Publishing, Fall 1987, p. 10
3. One example of how this new emphasis on the church has touched other continents is the book *Restoration in the Church* (Cityhill Publishing, 1989) by Terry Virgo. The author, a British pastor who heads a leadership team overseeing more than sixty nondenominational churches, describes the characteristics of a newly revitalized breed of churches that have reshaped the face of Christianity in Great Britain.

Chapter 3

1. Mark 12:30-31
2. Mark 12:33
3. David Matthew, *Church Adrift*, Marshall Morgan & Scott Ltd., 1985, p. 24-25.

Chapter 4

1. Eph. 3:14-15
2. Matthew, *Church Adrift*, p. 25
3. Ecc. 3:11
4. Rom. 13:8-10 (RSV)
5. Rom. 14:17 (RSV)
6. James 1:27

Chapter 5

1. Eph. 4:1
2. Eph. 5:1-2
3. Billy Graham, *Approaching Hoofbeats*, Key Word Books, 1985, p. 31
4. Eph. 4:16

5. Eph. 2:16
6. Rom. 6:5-6
7. Luke 9:23
8. Luke 14:27
9. John 17:23
10. John 15:12-13
11. John 15.15

Chapter 6

1. 1 Tim. 1:5

Chapter 7

1. Rom. 2:28-29
2. Matt. 3:9
3. John 8:44
4. Gal. 3:6,7,11,12
5. Gal. 4:30
6. John 5:39
7. Luke 24:27
8. Luke 24:45
9. Eph. 3:4-5
10. 1 Peter 1:11
11. Rom: 8:6 (NASB)
12. John 3:3
13. 1 Cor. 2:14
14. Col 2:16-17
15. John 3:14-15
16. "For God so loved the world that he gave his one and only Son, that whoever believes in him shall not perish but have eternal life."

Chapter 8

1. Note these scriptures, for example:
• "Out of all the peoples on the face of the earth, the Lord has

chosen you to be his treasured possession" (Deut. 14:2).

• "He has declared that he will set you in praise, fame and honor high above all the nations he has made and that you will be a people holy to the Lord your God, as he promised" (Deut. 26:19).

• "Sing with joy for Jacob; shout for the greatest of the nations" (Jer. 31:7).

• "You will be blessed more than any other people (Deut. 7:14).

2. Deut. 28:12-13

3. Lindsey, *Late Great Earth*, p. 33.

4. Edgar C. Whisenant, *On Borrowed Time: 88 Reasons Why the Rapture Could be in 1988*, World Bible Society, 1988, pp. 14.

5. *Christianity Today*, Oct. 21, 1988, p. 43.

6. Lindsey, *Late Great Earth*, p. 40.

7. Lindsey cites the "golden rule of interpretation" of Scripture, quoting this rule from David L. Cooper's book, *When God's Armies Meet the Almighty in the Land of Israel* (Biblical Research Society: Los Angeles, 1940): "When the plain sense of Scripture makes common sense, seek no other sense; therefore, take every word at its primary, ordinary, usual, literal meaning unless the facts of the immediate context, studies in the light of related passages and axiomatic and fundamental truths, indicate clearly otherwise."

8. Phil. 3:4-6

9. Phil. 3:9

10. Acts 21:28

11. "For not all who are descended from Israel are Israel. Nor because they are his descendants are they all Abraham's children. On the contrary, 'It is through Isaac that your offspring will be reckoned.' In other words, it is not the natural children who are God's children, but it is the children of the promise who are regarded as Abraham's offspring" (Rom. 9:6-8).

12. This passage goes on to explain in verses 2-18 that the law was inadequate because animal sacrifices could not atone for sin

Errata

Please note these corrections in the footnotes.

Chapter 8 footnotes

On page 245, footnote 13, the italics were inadvertently omitted. In the first paragraph quotation of 1 Tim. 3:15, the following words should be italicized: *which is the church of the living God*. In the third paragraph quotation of Heb. 3:5-6, the following should be italicized: *And we are his house*.

Chapter 9 footnotes

Footnotes for Chapter 9 (see pages 246-7) should read as follows:
1. Gal. 4: 24-25
2. David Pleggi, "Believers in Israel," *Charisma & Christian Life*, June 1989, p. 48.
3. Isa. 60:1-5, 7 (NKJV)
4. Deut. 26:19
5. 1 Chron. 22:5
6. Isa. 26:1-2
7. Isa. 60:14-15
8. Isa. 60:18,19, 21
9. Isa. 62:2-3
10. Zech. 8:23
11. Zech. 9:16-17
12. Micah 4:1-2 and Isa. 2:2-3
13. Isa. 60:15 (NKJV)
14. Isa. 46:11b (NKJV)

Chapter 18 footnotes

Footnote 3, page 249, should read Phil. 2:15.

and that God set that imperfect system aside when Jesus became the perfect sacrifice.

13. Paul made clear that the house of God was synonymous with the church in 1 Tim. 3:15 as well: ..."I write so that you may know how you ought to conduct yourself in the house of God, which is the church of the living God, the pillar and ground of the truth" (NKJ), (italics added).

Hebrews also states plainly that the tabernacle on earth is but a "shadow" of the true tabernacle: "We do have such a high priest, who sat down at the right hand of the throne of the Majesty in heaven, and who serves in the sanctuary, the true tabernacle set up by the Lord, not by man. . . . They [high priests on earth] serve at a sanctuary that is a copy and shadow of what is in heaven. This is why Moses was warned when he was about to build the tabernacle: 'See to it that you make everything according to the pattern shown you on the mountain'" (Heb. 8:1,2,5).

Elsewhere, Hebrews indicates that Moses' tabernacle was a sign of another tabernacle: the eternal, spiritual house of God, which is the church. "Moses was faithful as a servant in all God's house, testifying to what would be said in the future. But Christ is faithful as a son over God's house. And we are his house, if we hold on to our courage and the hope of which we boast" (Heb. 3:5-6, italics added).

14. Eph. 2:19-22

15. "As you come to him, the living Stone—rejected by men but chosen by God and precious to him—you also, like living stones, are being built into a spiritual house to be a holy priesthood, offering spiritual sacrifices acceptable to God through Jesus Christ" (1 Pet. 2:4,5).

16. "It was not through law that Abraham and his offspring received the promise that he would be heir of the world, but through the righteousness that comes by faith. For if those who live by law are heirs, faith has no value and the promise is worthless" (Rom. 4:13-14).

17. Gen 17:18 (NASB)

18. Gen. 17:19. See also Gen.21:12

19. Rom. 9:6

20. Rom. 9:8 (NASB)

21. Rom. 9:7 (NASB)

22. Gal. 4:28 (NKJV)

23. Gen. 25:23

24. Rom. 9:13. (NKJV) See also Malachi 1:2,3.

25. 1 Cor. 1:29 (NKJV)

26. 1 Cor. 15:50

27. Rom. 1:17 (NKJV)

28. Note, for example, this passage in Galatians: "Understand, then, that those who believe are children of Abraham. The Scripture foresaw that God would justify the Gentiles by faith, and announced the gospel in advance to Abraham: 'All nations will be blessed through you'" (Gal. 3:7-8).

29. Eph. 3:10-11

30. Col. 1:27

31. Note these scriptures:

• "They are the shoot I have planted, the work of my hands, for the display of my splendor" (Isaiah 60:21).

• "You lead your people, to make Yourself a glorious name" (Isa. 63:14, NKJV).

• "He said to me, "You are my servant, Israel, in whom I will display my splendor" (Isa. 49:3).

• "Break forth into singing, you mountains, O forest, and every tree in it! For the Lord has redeemed Jacob, and glorified Himself in Israel" (Isa. 44:23, NKJV).

• "I will grant salvation to Zion, my splendor to Israel" (Isa. 46:13).

32. Rom. 3:30

33. Rom. 10:12,13 (NKJV)

Chapter 9

1. Isa. 60:1-5,7 (NKJV)

2. David Pleggi, "Believers in Israel," *Charisma & Christian*

Life, June 1989, p. 48
3. Deut. 26:18-19
4. 1 Chron. 22:5
5. Isa. 26:1-2
6. Isa. 60:14-15
7. Isa. 60:18,19,21
8. Isa. 62:2-3
9. Zech. 8:23
10. Zech. 9:16-17
11. Micah 4:1-3 and Isa. 2:23
12. Isa. 60:15 (NKJV)
13. Isa. 46:11 (NKJV)
14. Isa. 46:116

Chapter 10

1. Prov. 29:18 (KJV)
2. Rom. 11:11
3. *Wall Street Journal*, Thursday, Aug. 22, 1985
4. Matt. 16:18
5. Jer. 32:27
6. C. H. Spurgeon, *The Treasury of David*, 1874, cited in Iain H. Murray, *The Puritan Hope, A Study in Revival and the Interpretation of Prophecy*, The Banner of Truth Trust, 1971, p. xiv. Used by permission. The excerpt was taken from an exposition of Psalm 86:9, "All nations whom thou hast made shall come and worship before thee, O Lord; and shall glorify thy name."
7. "I will pour out my Spirit on all people. Your sons and daughters will prophesy, your old men will dream dreams, your young men will see visions. Even on my servants, both men and women, I will pour out my Spirit in those days" (Joel 2:28-29).
8. Murray, *Puritan Hope*, p. 96. Additional excerpts from Puritan Hope appear in the appendix.
9. J.C.Ryle in "An Estimate of Thomas Manton," 1870, quoted in *Puritan Hope*, p. xxi-xxii.

Chapter 11

1. Heb. 11:10
2. John 12:24-25
3. Matt. 10:38
4. Mark 8:34
5. Luke 14:27
6. Psa. 69:9
7. Zech. 8:2 (NKJV)

Chapter 12

1. 1 Chron. 22:5
2. Isa. 2:2

Chapter 14

1. 1 Chron. 22:5
2. Luke 12:51-52
3. Mark 10:29

Chapter 15

1. 1 Chron. 22:5
2. Daniel 3

Chapter 16

1. Ps. 84:2
2. Ps. 42:1
3. Isa. 60:15
4. Phil. 3:7
5. 1 Cor. 14:12 (NKJV)
6. "Let the elders who rule well be counted worthy of double honor, especially those who labor in the word and doctrine" (1 Tim. 5:17 NKJV).

Chapter 17

1. Jerry White, "The Disciples' Place in the Local Church," *Discipleship Journal*, Issue 35, Sept./Oct. 1986, pp.22-25.
2. White, *Discipleship Journal*, p. 22-25
3. 1 Cor. 16:1-3
4. Mal. 3:10 (NKJV)
5. C.F. Keil & F. Delitzsch, *Commentary on the Old Testament*, Erdmans Publishing Co: Grand Rapids, Mich., 1980, Vol. 10, p. 463. In their commentary on Malachi 3:10, they say, "The emphasis lies upon kol; the whole of the tithe they are to bring, and not merely a portion of it, and so defraud the Lord."
6. Leighton Ford, "Evangelism Into the 21st Century," World Vision, February-March 1989, p. 6

Chapter 18

1. Rom. 1:20
2. Ps. 14:1
3. Phil. 2:14
4. Neh. 2:17
5. This story appears in Judges, chapter 7.

Also from Cityhill...

Lives in Focus
Profiles of Struggle and Strength

Edited by Richard Myhre

Going beyond outdated tracts, this book presents with compelling candor stories of fourteen ordinary men and women whose lives have been changed.

Some passed through trying terrain. A childhood spent wishing for a "normal" family. A disintegrating career. A marriage collapse. Others came of age in the '60s with all its causes, questions, and contradictions. Each person shares the obstacles they encountered and the solutions they found.

Written in a contemporary, non-religious style, *Lives in Focus* is a non-threatening evangelistic tool for Christians who want to creatively communicate the gospel to their co-workers, neighbors, family members, and friends.

Available from your local Christian bookstore or by sending $3.95 plus $1 for shipping to:

Cityhill Publishing
4600 Christian Fellowship Road
Columbia, MO 65203

Also from Cityhill...

On To Maturity
Maintaining Spiritual Momentum
By Arthur Wallis

This practical study course, a sequel to Wallis' *Living God's Way*, is designed to help propel Christians forward in their walk with God. It has eighteen lessons, complete with memory verses and homework assignments, which apply Bible truths to the challenges you face every day. Topics include:
•Dealing with resentment
•Controlling your emotions
•The Christian in the workplace
•Resisting temptation
•Finding God's will

Available from your local Christian bookstore or by sending $4.95 plus $1 for shipping to:

Cityhill Publishing
4600 Christian Fellowship Road
Columbia, MO 65203